Jean Rhys

Twayne's English Authors Series

Kinley Roby, Editor

TEAS 536

JEAN RHYS
Photo by Ander Gunn

Jean Rhys

Sanford Sternlicht

Syracuse University

Twayne Publishers
An Imprint of Simon & Schuster Macmillan
New York

Prentice Hall International
London • Mexico City • New Delhi • Singapore • Sydney • Toronto

Twayne's English Authors Series No. 536

Jean Rhys
Sanford Sternlicht

Twayne Publishers
An Imprint of Simon & Schuster Macmillan
1633 Broadway
New York, NY 10019–6785

Library of Congress Cataloging-in-Publication Data

Sternlicht, Sanford V.
    Jean Rhys / Sanford Sternlicht.
        p.   cm.—(Twayne's English authors series : no. 536)
    Includes bibliographical references and index.
    ISBN 0–8057–4607–2 (alk. paper)
    1. Rhys, Jean—Criticism and interpretation.   2. Autobiographical
fiction, English—History and criticism.   3. Women and literature—
England—History—20th century.   4. Caribbean Area—In literature.
5. West Indies—In literature.   I. Title.   II. Series: Twayne's
English authors series ; TEAS 536.
PR6035.H96Z88   1997
823′.912—dc21   96–46388
                                                                CIP

10 9 8 7 6 5 4 3 2 1

Printed in the United States of America

to granddaughter Rachel

Contents

Preface

Dying just a few months before her ninetieth birthday, Jean Rhys lived a long, full, bitter, and tumultuous life. Her triumph as a literary artist came almost too late. Jean Rhys was a woman who truly loved men, from her father and the lovers of her youth to her third and last husband. Most of them disappointed, used, abandoned, or betrayed her. None gave her all of the three things she desperately sought in life: peace, security, and emotional support. I suppose that Rhys believed that men should have provided the necessary support for the gentility that she assumed was her birthright as daughter of a colonial island's ruling class, a birthright that she, of course, abandoned herself when she chose self-exile. In her frustrations Rhys grew angry and paranoid. She struck out or chose passive aggression, she drank, and she raged at life and everyone within range. But simply put, her deep disappointment was the source of her art.

Jean Rhys is one of the twentieth century's exile writers, like Joyce, Lawrence, Mann, Brecht, Beckett, and so many others. She was born West Indian white Creole; she found her art in Paris and in the values and techniques of French modernist fiction; and she lived most of her life in England, a country she despised because of its seeming misogyny, stuffiness, and coldness, let alone its most un–West Indian weather.

Now Jean Rhys is recognized as a major modernist writer, one who in the production of texts is disposed to see life as a fragmentary, complex, disjointed experience; who conflates memory, history, and momentary sensations to produce impressionistic, multivoiced texts imbued with a dark if not despairing ambiguity; who sees words as actions; who valorizes style as the penultimate value in creative writing; who often foregrounds a disguised coterie for the voyeuristic pleasure of the cognoscenti; who, in the existentialist mode, assumes the loneliness of the individual and the impossibility of complete communication between people; who is a self-exile from a country, a culture, or a class; who has cognizance of Freudian thought and employs a knowledge (second or third hand perhaps) of psychoanalytic theory; and who is scornful of the values and norms of bourgeois society and the fabrications of popular culture. Simultaneously, and perhaps most significantly, Jean Rhys is one of the major voices of feminine consciousness in the twentieth century.

Jean Rhys's fiction presents a major modernist and feminist narrative in which, although composing in the codes of the dominant mode, she nevertheless brilliantly subverts the master narrative. Jean Rhys seemingly created a significant body of fiction out of her own flesh and blood. In her first four novels she takes a woman on a mythic yet personal early twentieth-century journey from youth to middle age. Even in her masterpiece, *Wide Sargasso Sea*, her one novel set in the nineteenth century, she created art out of painful personal experience and developed an enduring portrait of Western woman as the marginalized Other, stripped of identity, seeking only peace and safety but driven by the controlling Patriarchal forces of her time to morbid passivity, passive aggression, and sometimes violent rage. The moving picture of a woman's decay into self-pity, self-contempt, and even to madness is real and ugly. No wonder the reading of and discourse on the works of Jean Rhys have become so central to contemporary feminist literary study.

Jean Rhys begins with an up-to-date biographical sketch made possible by two very recent superb studies, the outstanding biography *Jean Rhys: Life and Work* (1990) by Carole Angier and the superlative biographical-critical study *Jean Rhys* (1991) by Coral Ann Howells. Scholars, students, and other readers of Jean Rhys must be warned that pre-1990 sources of biographical information are replete with errors. In her long lifetime Jean Rhys lied, hid, covered, and forgot. *Jean Rhys* proceeds to evaluate the author's work in chronological order of publication, to indicate her stylistic development, and from several contemporary critical perspectives, including feminist literary theory, post-colonial literary criticism, and intertextuality discourse, the latter two approaches in regard, especially, to *Wide Sargasso Sea* as prequel and angry response to *Jane Eyre*.

Several people at Syracuse University deserve my thanks: Dr. Wendy Bousfield; my excellent undergraduate research assistants Sheila Dougherty and Brian T. Lammana; the patient, friendly staff of the Faculty Support Center, and the ever capable interlibrary loan staff of Bird Library.

The following have generously given permission to quote from Jean Rhys's work: W. W. Norton for quotes from *Wide Sargasso Sea* (copyright 1966 by Jean Rhys); HarperCollins Publishers for quotes from *Quartet* and *After Leaving Mr. MacKenzie*; and Penguin Books for quotes from *Voyage in the Dark* (Penguin Books 1969, first published by Constable) and *Good Morning, Midnight* (Penguin Books 1969, first published by Constable), "reproduced by permission of Penguin Books Ltd."

I wish to thank Francis Wyndham, Jean Rhys's literary executor, and the Department of Special Collections of the McFarlin Library, University of Tulsa, for permission to use the frontispiece photograph of Jean Rhys. Also thanks to Lori N. Curtis, Associate Curator of Special Collections at McFarlin Library, for her great patience in locating the photograph and helping me in the permission process.

Sanford Sternlicht
Syracuse, New York

Chronology

1890 Born Ella Gwendoline Rees Williams 24 August at Roseau, Dominica, to Minna Lockhart Rees Williams and Dr. William Rees Williams. Third of five surviving children.

1907 Sent to England for schooling at Pearse School for Girls, Cambridge.

1909 Enrolls in Academy of Dramatic Art for two terms. Father withdraws her after unpromising report.

1910 Chorus Girl. Father dies in Dominica. Affair with wealthy stockbroker Lancelot Smith.

1912 Dropped by Smith. Demimondaine existence.

1913 Nearly dies from late-term abortion.

1914 Model. Engaged to *London Times* correspondent Maxwell Macartney.

1917 Macartney breaks off engagement.

1919 Marries Willem "John" Lenglet, Dutch spy, journalist, and writer, in The Hague. Move to Paris. First child dies at three months of age.

1920 Lenglets move to Vienna, then Budapest. Flee the law.

1922 Daughter, Maryvonne, born in Ukkel, Belgium.

1923 Family in Paris.

1924 Meets Ford Madox Ford. They become lovers. Ella Rees Williams becomes Jean Rhys. Ford publishes her in *Transatlantic Review*.

1925 Lenglet imprisoned for theft and deported. Rhys stays in Paris.

1927 Affair with Ford ends. Rhys begins life-long heavy drinking. Meets Leslie Tilden Smith, literary agent, in London. *The Left Bank and Other Stories.*

1928 Mother dies in London. Begins living there with Tilden Smith. *Postures*, published as *Quartet* next year.

1931 *After Leaving Mr. Mackenzie.*

1933 Divorced from Lenglet.

1934 Marries Tilden Smith. *Voyage in the Dark.*

1936 Visit to Dominica.

1939 *Good Morning, Midnight.* Last publication for 25 years.

1945 Tilden Smith dies.

1946 Moves into Beckenham, London house of Tilden Smith's cousin, Max Hamer, solicitor.

1947 Marries Max Hamer.

1949 Rhys arrested for assaulting neighbors and police in Beckenham. Sent to Holloway Prison Hospital, London, for psychiatric evaluation. Released and placed on probation. Actress Selma vaz Dias "finds" Rhys and begins long, troubled friendship and professional relationship.

1950 Hamer imprisoned for two years for larceny.

1957 Vaz Dias "finds" Rhys again, for BBC radio production of *Good Morning, Midnight.* Rhys begins to write once more.

1960 Jean and Max move into last home at Cheriton Fitzpaine, Devonshire.

1964 Hamer dies.

1966 *Wide Sargasso Sea.* Fellow, Royal Society of Literature.

1967 André Deutsch commences reissuing Rhys's novels.

1968 *Tigers Are Better-Looking* (stories).

1976 *Sleep It Off, Lady* (stories).

1978 Awarded C.B.E. (Commander, Order of the British Empire).

1979 Dies in Royal Devon and Exeter Hospital, 14 May. *Smile Please: An Unfinished Autobiography.*

1981 Film *Quartet* adapted by James Ivory and Ruth Prawer Jhabvala.

1993 Film *Wide Sargasso Sea* adapted by Jan Sharp, Carole Angier, and John Duigan.

Chapter One

A Woman's Life

Childhood and Adolescence

Ella Gwendoline Rees Williams was born on 24 August 1890, at Roseau, Dominica, the Windward Islands (part of the Leeward Islands configuration at that time), Lesser Antilles, West Indies. Dominica, roughly 30 miles long, 10 miles wide, and 290 square miles, is the largest of the Windward Islands, and Roseau is its capital. It is a mountainous, rain-forested island almost devoid of the usual white sand beaches in the Caribbean. Once a French possession (and thus the place names and the patois), the British colonized it from the end of the eighteenth century until independence in 1978.

Her father, Dr. William Rees Williams, an immigrant from Wales in 1881, was medical officer and health officer to the port of Roseau.[1] In 1882 he married Minna Lockhart, whose family was one of the fourth generations of white Creole plantation owners and whose ancestor, the Scot James Potter Lockhart, had bought the Geneva Plantation on Grand Bay in 1824, a property of over one thousand sugar-growing acres replete with more than two hundred slaves. Ten years later the British emancipation of slaves destroyed the plantation way of life, and ten years after emancipation the former slaves burned down the manor house. The less resplendent, rebuilt house was burned down in the early 1930s, a few years before Jean's one and only visit to her homeland after she left for England in 1907.

Despite the Scottish name, James's wife, Jean Maxwell, came from Cuba and may have been Spanish. She was always described as "dark" and possibly had some African blood (Angier, 7). Whatever the bloodlines, to Jean Rhys, there was no English in this "English" colonial girl's background.

Minna and William had six children, five of whom survived infancy. Jean was the fifth child. Before Jean, a sister born 18 months earlier died of dysentery at the age of six months. Jean seems to have been a replacement child to ease her mother's grief, but Jean may have felt her

1

mother's sorrow and thought that Minna's occasional need for distance and grieving was caused by disappointment in her. She believed her parents loved her siblings more, especially her younger sister, Brenda, born in 1895, with whom she had a lifelong sibling rivalry. Her brothers and sisters were dark; she was fair. Late in life Jean told of an incident when she was given a fair doll and her sister a dark one, and Jean, wanting the dark one, the seemingly more acceptable one, smashed her fair doll to pieces. Being fair-haired and skinned made Jean, in her own sensitive eyes, different not only from her siblings but also from the Black people who worked the plantations, took care of her, and whom she saw as powerful, zestful, and mysterious (Angier, 15).

Jean loved her father intensely but saw him as powerful and remote. He seems to have genuinely cared for her and to have given her a proportionate amount of time considering his large family and professional obligations. He also purchased and administered two small estates in addition to the inheritance that had come to Minna. Jean's mother was the disciplinarian and was often physically harsh with her daughter.

Jean's first schooling was at the local Roman Catholic convent school, part of the time as a boarder. The instruction was largely in French, thus providing the young girl with a bilingualism that would ease her entry into Paris life later on and, of great significance to Rhys the writer, open access to early modern French literature (Angier, 20–21). Jean loved the nuns, especially the superior, Mother Mount Calvary, and she adored the glorious Catholic cathedral that was both more beautiful and more impressive than the Anglican Church of her parents and the island's "English" elite.

Blacks were the majority of parishioners in the Catholic church, and Jean was intrigued and fascinated by them. All her life Jean had ambiguous feelings toward Blacks: they were frightening and hostile; they were friendly and earthy; and, later, in Europe, as an alienated woman and an exile from the Caribbean, she could relate to them as other marginalized people (Angier, 13–14, 20, 656).

In her wonder and confusion the child wanted very much to become a nun. Her worried parents eventually decided that she would have to have further, nonreligious education in England. While at the convent school Jean commenced her lifelong love of reading and of books, devouring English romances and mysteries: Scott's novels, the Brontës, the Sherlock Holmes stories, and so forth. England became her Oz, the wonderful, beautiful, magical land of lords and ladies, stately homes, and gorgeous vistas, while London had to be the grandest of capitals.

Her early engrossment in English fiction instilled in Jean a deep respect for the escapist function of the narrative as well as an admiration for the power of the story to record, redefine, and relieve the sufferings of experience. But English fiction later caused the colonial girl in England great disappointment. Her beloved books, with their romantic values and archaic descriptions, made her vulnerable and, in a sense, betrayed her, while the reality of fast-paced, aggressive, competitive, industrialized Edwardian England shocked her into a dislike of the country and its people.

Before Rhys left Dominica, however, two sexual incidents occurred that disturbed her very much and that had long-lasting effects on her life. When Jean was about 12 or 13, her mother, surely unwittingly, allowed an elderly family friend to have the opportunity to sexually abuse the child. Jean was manipulated by the handsome, elderly gentleman, through attention, long walks together, flattery, romantic and sexual narratives, and treats, into allowing him to fondle her breasts.[2] She was "drugged" by the relationship with the clever, manipulating old father-lover figure.

Jean never told her parents, although her mother may have surmised what had occurred, because the family friend became less welcome in the Williams's home. Jean felt confused, guilty, and sinful because she found both fear and pleasure in the encounters, even exhilaration in the control the old man had over her body and her imagination, and although she was able to repress the guilt and the horrible feeling that she was evil, the experience contributed to her extreme passivity in sexual relations later, especially with older men, as well as to her lack of strength in emotional matters and her frequent denial of self-worth (Howells, 14).

Jean's first love affair and probably first sexual intercourse occurred when she was 16. The young man was 21, half white and half Carib Indian with some Black blood. The relationship was passionate but dangerous. They had violated a taboo and they knew it. Found out, they were quickly separated and kept apart (Angier, 31–33). Eighteen months later Rhys's West Indies days were over, as she was on her way to England to sojourn with Aunt Clarise, who became her surrogate mother in England, and to continue her schooling at the Pearse School for Girls in Cambridge, which she attended from 1907 to the end of 1908.

In her exile Rhys revealed an obsession with her first and perhaps only real home, possibly because she left her island at the early and difficult age between childhood and womanhood, and because she left with conflicts, emotional and sexual, not resolved and self-esteem not established.[3] It may be that very late in her life she was able, through *Wide Sargasso Sea,* to write her way back to Dominica and close the chapter of her childhood.

Except for acting in the school plays, Rhys did not like the life of a boarder at the Pearse School. Determined to be an actress, the 18-year-old girl was tutored in elocution and then sat for and passed the entrance examination to the Academy of Dramatic Art, later called the Royal Academy of Dramatic Art but in Rhys's time familiarly known as Tree's school, after its founder, the great English actor Sir Herbert Beerbohm Tree. Her father was supportive at first and provided the necessary funds, and she began study in January of 1909 (Angier, 44).

Rhys spent only two terms at the Academy. Her West Indian dialect was a severe handicap, and she did not show a great deal of talent. When this was reported to Dr. Williams, he withdrew his financial support of the schooling, and she had to give it up.

Rhys refused to return to Dominica as a "failure" even though her parents desired that she do so. Instead, she was determined to go on the stage, and apparently her liberal parents indulged her. On 19 June 1910, however, her father died suddenly of a heart attack, and Rhys needed to earn her own money (Angier, 49).

Striking Out on Her Own

Even before her father died, the resolute Rhys won a part. Early in 1909, fresh from Tree's school, she appeared in the chorus of the northern touring company of the popular London musical *Our Miss Gibbs,* using the stage name of Ella Gray. Other engagements followed. Rhys was free, beautiful, and living with other girls who were also attractive and ill educated. Although life on the theatrical road was hard (dingy rooming houses, bad food, poor pay, insufficient money spent on required clothes and makeup), she was young and happy. She loved the illusion of the theater. All her life Rhys was attracted by the surface, the superficial, a trait and a weakness that caused her much misery and suffering (Howells, 27).

Her dream was the dream of all the chorus girls and other young women of the demimonde: the Cinderella dream of winning the love of one of the many rich stage door Johnnies who hung around the theater and sexually feasted on the unsophisticated young actresses and chorus girls. With luck and skill, and there was some precedence for this, a girl might end up married and respectable. But the men had all the power and the choice. They wanted sex and seemed, perhaps neurotically, to enjoy it more freely with young girls of a lower class. Most expected to marry eventually into their own class in support of family interests and to provide heirs to the family fortunes.

The inexperienced Rhys thought she had reached the great goal when, at a supper party, she met and later became the lover of a rich stockbroker 20 years her senior, Lancelot Smith (Angier, 61, 64). He was an exploiter, of course, but he did have some conscience and a heart, and ultimately he may have given Rhys her material. He "kept" her for two years and probably thought all the time that he was helping her with her theatrical career, seeing that she had enough to eat and enough money to buy the lovely and expensive clothes Rhys adored. Like the old gentleman on Dominica, he was old enough to be her father, and with Dr. Williams dead, surely the role of surrogate father was one the sometimes homesick and usually lonely girl cast him in.

In the autumn of 1912 Smith dropped Rhys when he began a voyage to the United States (Angier, 69–70). It was only an excuse to put some distance between her and him when she received the devastating news by letter. He may have been the great love of her life, and his affluence, generosity, good breeding, and manners set a standard that none of Rhys's future lovers and husbands could match.

Rhys was emotionally distraught over the sudden betrayal. She became extremely ill and even suicidal. Quickly she became mistress to another less kind, sensitive, gentle, and generous man. He was of the rougher sort, and he soon dropped her, too. She began to pick up men, and in the life of a demimondaine, became a selective prostitute.

Rhys does not seem to have placed much significance on the sexual act itself, perhaps because she was reared on a tropical island among free-spirited agricultural workers and because she had early sexual experience. She sometimes used sex to obtain money, security, and professional aid. Mostly, however, she gave herself freely in love, sadly knowing that the gift would tire the receiver sooner or later. One wonders if she ever enjoyed sex with her middle-aged Victorian men, such as Smith and later Ford Madox Ford. She loved these portly gentlemen as father surrogates, but they were seeking validation, renewal, trophies, and fantasy incest with dependent child-daughters. She was dependent but not a child, and the men involved would eventually go on to other, younger, less troublesome conquests.

Smith continued to help Rhys a little financially for six years, but in early 1913 she became pregnant from her last lover or a client. With few friends and not daring to call on relatives for help in her predicament and "disgrace," the 23-year-old woman did not know what to do. At first she planned to go through with the pregnancy, and contacting Smith, she found him supportive. But he soon thought differently, and working through a surrogate, Smith talked her out of having the child and provided money for an illegal abortion (Angier, 76). Perhaps he was afraid that she would accuse him of fathering her child, and indeed she may have come to think, impossible though it was, that the child was his. In a sense the "progeny" from Rhys's and Smith's twisted, painful relationship was the character Walter in *Voyage in the Dark,* or perhaps the tortured text itself. Rhys had a late-term abortion, and she nearly died from the dangerous operation. She planned to commit suicide at Christmas, 1913, but fortunately a girlfriend talked her out of it, and slowly Rhys recommitted to life (Angier, 78–79).

Perhaps not coincidentally, Rhys began at this moment to write. Passing a stationery store window she was attracted by some colored pens. She bought them and some other writing supplies, including several black exercise books. At home she began to write down the things that had happened to her in her life. It felt very good. Rhys learned that writing could assuage the pain of her heartbreaks. Indeed, it could be purgative, but it could also intensify the pleasure of the high times of her life. She wrote sporadically but did not discard her work. These diary-like accounts would serve as the notebook source of much of Rhys's early fiction. Her slim figure and good looks got her work as an artist's model, and she became a fringe member of English Bohemia. She also returned to stage work, but just as she got employment, the outbreak of World War I in 1914 caused all the theaters to be closed.

Bohemian Life and First Marriage

Meanwhile Rhys had met the London *Times* reporter Maxwell Macartney in one of Soho's Bohemian haunts, and they soon were engaged to be married (Angier, 84). But the relationship was not a warm one; in many ways they were ill suited. Rhys was beautiful and desirable, a trophy for the bookish Macartney, but he was an intellectual, and Rhys was poorly educated. She tried to narrow the cultural gap by reading his books: Hardy, Conrad, Galsworthy, Bennett, and the plays of Shaw. Macartney quickly went off to France to report the war, leaving Rhys bewildered.

At least she had rediscovered her childhood pleasure and solace: reading. Now she was reading some of the best living English writers of the time. Macartney returned in 1917 to renew the engagement, but just as Rhys was planning the marriage, he suddenly broke it off (Angier, 94–95). Rhys was stunned and then furious over yet another betrayal, but she found it impossible to confront these betrayers. After all, they had all the power and they were father-authority figures. She internalized much of her anger and relieved it by commencing a pattern of passive-aggressive behavior. She also began to find alcohol helpful for numbing psychological misery. She felt at least partly responsible for her losses, not knowing that Macartney was the type of man who appeared to collect engagements, getting cold feet again and again when the actual marriage loomed (Angier, 95).

Late in 1917, in her rooming house, Rhys met Willem Lenglet, a Dutchman employed as a spy for the French government (Angier, 97). He was one year older than Rhys but thought he was five, because Rhys had already begun to take four years off her true age. He called himself Jean Lenglet, and Rhys always called him John. He was witty, exciting, personable, very attentive, and aggressive. He also was married, but Rhys did not know that. In fact he had been married twice, divorced only once, and had a son by his first wife. Lenglet courted Rhys fiercely, and a few weeks after they met, and before they had even kissed, he proposed marriage, and she accepted (Angier, 99).

Lenglet had to leave immediately for Holland, and because of the war, Rhys was unable to go to him until April 1919 (Angier, 103). They were married in The Hague on 30 April 1919. Lenglet did not divorce his second wife until six years later. He eventually became a journalist and a writer of fiction, but at the time of his marriage he had no real employment. For most of her married life with Lenglet, Rhys never knew or asked where the money he obtained came from. The young couple borrowed some money and made their way to Paris, the one city Rhys fell in love with and remained faithful to even in memory (Angier, 107). Until the last part of her creative life, the City of Light was her chief inspirational locale.

In Paris Rhys obtained a position as an English tutor to the children in an affluent French Jewish family, the Richelots. One member of the Richelot family, Germaine Richelot, became Rhys's long-term friend and generous financial helper until the beginning of World War II in 1939 and the disappearance of the family during the German occupation. Because she was pregnant, Rhys only worked for the Richelots for a few months.

William Owen Lenglet was born on 29 December 1919. Three weeks later, the child was ill and in the hospital. On 19 January 1920 the child died there of pneumonia while his parents were at home drinking with friends (Angier, 113). They did not know their child had died until the next day. Believing that she had not taken care of her infant adequately, Rhys was racked with guilt, and she suffered from the memory of the loss of her son all her life.

In March 1920 the Lenglets moved to Vienna, where John, a skilled linguist, had obtained a position with the Japanese delegation to the Interallied Commission, an organization that oversaw the disarmament of the former Austro-Hungarian Empire (Angier, 114). Appearing four years later in Ford Madox Ford's *Transatlantic Review,* Rhys's first published story, "Vienne," is set there. Rhys was in one of the happiest periods of her life. The commission soon moved to the other capital of the ex-empire, Budapest, and the Lenglets moved too, with Rhys enjoying that city even more than Vienna (Angier, 118).

But Lenglet had the spy's subversive mind, and he loved money. Somehow, without informing his wife, of course, he became involved in illegal money trafficking. He believed he was about to be apprehended, and so, late in 1921, the couple fled Hungary in the night (Angier, 120). In fact Lenglet was never arrested for those misdeeds, whatever they were, but the threat must have been quite palpable to provoke a desperate, panicked flight. Rhys was pregnant at the time, too.

In Ukkel, near Brussels, on 22 May 1922, Rhys delivered an infant girl, Maryvonne, her only child to survive infancy (Angier, 121). In the summer they moved to Paris again. The Lenglets were broke, they had an infant, and John, convinced that there was a Hungarian warrant for his arrest, did not register with the French authorities and thus had no legal papers with which to find work. The Lenglets were not good parents. Maryvonne spent much of her early life in charitable institutions and foster care. Some of her childhood was spent in France and some in Holland. Germaine Richelot helped them, and once, just before the trip to Paris, Rhys dashed to London and cadged some money from Smith, perhaps with his admonition that this would be the last time he would see her or help her.

Mother and daughter had an on-again, off-again relationship for the rest of Rhys's life. The often neglected Maryvonne never believed that her mother loved her in the primary way children expect. Rhys, of course, loved good times, adventures, luxury, and alcohol above the restricting duties of motherhood, and when, later, she was seriously committed to writing, her work took precedence over parental responsibilities. For much of Maryvonne's childhood, her rival was Rhys's work. Maryvonne Moerman currently lives in the Netherlands. She too has a daughter.

Ford Madox Ford

Lenglet wrote journalistic pieces and Rhys translated them into English. Trying to raise some money by selling the translations to English language publications, Rhys showed them to a friend, Mrs. H. Pearl Adam, whom she had met in London before 1914 and with whom she was staying while Lenglet was away for a few days. Adam's husband, George Adam, had been the London *Times* correspondent in Paris and was now working for several U.S. papers, and thus he was a good contact for the possible sale of Lenglet's and Rhys's material. But Pearl asked Rhys to see some of her own work, and she was shown the journals Rhys had been keeping (Angier, 130).

Adam was impressed with her young friend's writing. She did some organizing and editing and then showed the material to the English novelist Ford Madox Ford, who had edited *The English Review* early in the century, and who was then residing in Paris with the *avant garde*, working on his magnum opus, *Parade's End*, and editing the distinguished, if short-lived, *Transatlantic Review*, which published Joyce, Hemingway, Pound, Gertrude Stein, Dorothy Richardson, Picasso, Djuna Barnes, Nancy Cunard, Mina Loy, Joseph Conrad, Paul Valéry, and other young modernists (Howells, 25). Rhys had probably not heard of Ford[4] or many of his expatriate literary associates, but she could only have been happy that an editor thought her work very interesting and promising. As was Ford's wont, especially if the neophyte was a young and attractive woman, he undertook to tutor her in the writing of fiction. When in 1924 he was about to published her story "Vienne," he suggested that she adopt a pen name, and so Ella Lenglet became Jean Rhys (Angier, 138). Interestingly, she created her new identity from her pet name for her husband, "John," and from a version of her father's middle name, "Rees." Was the name meant to appear androgynous? Did she believe that since she was writing in and about Paris, some would think she was a French man? Did she think it would hide her, or give her an edge, or more serious attention if she were taken for a male writer? Was she psychologically sheltering herself under patriarchal wings, hoping for approval from husband and even dead father?

To Rhys's great shock, her husband was arrested on 28 December 1924, for theft. Apparently he had stolen a considerable sum of money from the travel agency for which he worked. (During all of her three marriages, Rhys seems to have been oblivious as to the source of her husbands' income and their work.) Lenglet was convicted and sentenced to imprisonment for eight months on 10 February 1925, with the understanding that he would be deported upon release. Freed early, he was deported to the Netherlands in June (Angier, 124–28). Rhys was without a husband but she was not alone. She had become Ford's lover.

Rhys must have had a fierce father fixation. Ford was 50 years old, fat, and had a scraggly blond mustache. She was 34, slender, and lovely. She still looked the ingenue. Odd that a woman who disliked England so always fell for the English gentleman type. Ford was hardly that, but he put on a good and very successful act with strangers, especially young women. Still, Ford was a great teacher, and he taught her well. Rhys must have realized that she had a unique opportunity to learn an art from a master, and love and sex may have been seen as both a fair and necessary payment.

Ford set her to writing short stories. He explained and demonstrated the form, and he did not condescend because she was a woman. In his introduction to *The Left Bank* Ford noted that Rhys had "an instinct for form."[5] He helped her to develop a clear, cool, lean, and distinctive narrative voice, controlled and dispassionate despite subjectivity and the autobiographical material (Howells, 29). Without knowing the term, Rhys embraced that key modernist concept of the *objective correlative* as she let the narrative action, not the persona, "speak" the emotion. It was for the reader to set the emotional distance from the text. Rhys learned to value precision and economy over everything else in writing.

Ford took her everywhere and introduced her to everyone. She became known as "Ford's Girl." Rhys sober was ladylike and diffident, showing her island "aristocratic" breeding, and she always had a very soft speaking voice, except, of course, when she was in a rage. Few if any of the artists and writers of the "lost generation" Rhys met in the Paris of the 1920s knew that the quiet, beautiful, observing woman was a writer. In fact Rhys was never truly a part of any literary scene. She was always on the margin or outside.

Of course Ford already had a lover, one without a husband, absent or not. He was living with the Australian painter Stella Bowen. Stella was more than a lover; she was his common-law wife. Ford tried to keep the relationship with Rhys secret from Bowen, but naturally she found out.

Rhys's need was great. Ford was exploitative, manipulative, and controlling. He talked both Bowen and Rhys into consenting to a ménage à trois. The story of this triangular affair plus a husband became Rhys's first novel, *Quartet*. Ford and Lenglet would also fictionalize it and Bowen would write about it, too, in her autobiography, *Drawn from Life*. In six months or so Ford was tired of Rhys and was ready to get rid of her.[6]

In 1926 Ford obtained a job for Rhys in the south of France ghost-writing for a rich American woman, Mrs. Richard Hudnut (Angier, 147–49). Rhys was happy because she was physically comfortable in a rich woman's home, but oddly, and perhaps because he wanted Rhys back for a while, Ford fouled the job for her with a letter to Rhys's patron stating that she was taking advantage of her resident writer. Rhys was astonished to be let go, and she sadly returned to Paris. Bowen did not want her living with them and so Ford got Rhys a small apartment. Rhys knew that Ford had lost interest in her sexually, and she was alone and miserable. Her deep alcoholism stems from this period. Although Lenglet never quite forgave Rhys for her affair with Ford while he was in prison, he did arrange for her to move to Holland with him and to reestablish the family with Maryvonne (Angier, 157).

Ford still wished to help Rhys the writer, or perhaps he still had some feelings for her, romantic or erotic, so he arranged for her to translate, from French to English, *Perversité,* written by Francis Carco and published by Pascal Covici, who fraudulently issued the book as translated by Ford because he believed it would sell better under the famous name (Angier, 164). Ford had nothing to do with the decision, but Rhys, suspicious of the manipulations of the men in her life, and for good reason, assumed he had tricked and betrayed her again. From that time on there was bad blood between them, even though he helped her to bring out *The Left Bank* in 1927 with his laudatory (if also self-serving) introduction. Rhys's ultimate revenge was her portrayal of Ford as two rather odious characters, Heidler in *Quartet* and the eponymous Mr. Mackenzie.

First Publications and Second Marriage

In late 1927 the Lenglet family moved to The Hague (Angier, 171). Rhys would never again live in Paris, the beautiful and beloved city of her earliest inspiration; her brief and giddy whirl around the fringe of the "greats" of the lost generation; and her first success as a writer. For a few years to come she would visit Paris when she could afford to, alone, to recharge creativity and reabsorb the city's atmosphere.

In December 1927 Rhys's mother was dying in London and Rhys went to say good-bye. Minna Williams died in January 1928, and Rhys was at the funeral, where she fought with her sister Brenda (Angier, 227). She also met or met again the literary agent and publishers' reader, Leslie Tilden Smith. It is possible that she first became acquainted with him in 1926 during a brief trip to London to arrange for the publication of *The Left Bank* with Jonathan Cape. Rhys's marriage to Lenglet was for all practical purposes over. They had stayed together for Maryvonne's sake and to pool their meager incomes, scratched out from writing and whatever else they could do to bring in a little money. Now Rhys fell in love with Tilden Smith, another English gentleman type: he was well spoken, an Oxford graduate, divorced, and he had grown children. Rhys moved in with him in his London flat (Angier, 232).

Tilden Smith was a quiet, gentle man who had been a World War I Royal Flying Corps pilot. He failed as a literary agent and eked out a paltry subsistence as a reader for several publishers. He genuinely loved Rhys, appreciated and admired her great ability as a writer, served as her agent, typed her manuscripts, provided the support system for the difficult, hard-drinking artist, and was generally unappreciated by Rhys. He would appear in her work only as a minor character, George Horsfield, in *After Leaving Mr. Mackenzie*. It was in his company, particularly during the 1928–39 period, that, after all, the bulk of Rhys's work was written and published, and even *Wide Sargasso Sea* was conceived.

In 1928 Cape published *Postures*. Rhys's original title was *Quartet*, but the publishers, fearing a libel suit by Ford, thought that *Postures* somehow was a safer title. All subsequent publications of the novel were as *Quartet*. In 1931 *After Leaving Mr. Mackenzie* was published. Meanwhile Maryvonne had been shuttling between Holland and England. Finally Lenglet asked for a divorce and custody of the girl (Angier, 236). Rhys agreed that, at the child's request, Maryvonne should reside permanently with her father and spend only holidays with her mother and Tilden Smith. Rhys simply preferred writing and drinking to motherhood. Lenglet then grew reluctant to grant Rhys the divorce she now desired, perhaps because he still cared for her, or because he selfishly wanted a new partner first (Angier, 290). When he found one early in 1933, he allowed the divorce to proceed, and in September Rhys was free, although, ironically she could have had her marriage to Lenglet annulled at any time because he had not divorced his second wife when Rhys and he exchanged vows.

In 1932 Rhys did an extraordinarily generous thing for Lenglet. She translated into English and edited, shaped, and cut his unpublished French novel about their days with Ford and Bowen, *Sous les Verrous,* brought out as *Barred* (Angier, 287). She worked harder to get it published than she ever did for her own work, and she succeeded. The novel was well reviewed, and after publication in Holland and France, it led to Lenglet's acceptance as a serious writer.

Rhys and Tilden Smith were married on 19 February 1934, and *Voyage in the Dark*, painfully finished by a heavy-drinking Rhys and typed by Tilden Smith, was published later that year (Angier, 292). At the time of their marriage Rhys was forty-three and Tilden Smith was forty-eight. It was the height of the Depression, and Tilden Smith was falling into bankruptcy. They were broke. Rhys had to beg small sums of money from family and keep writing. Prior to the publication of *Wide Sargasso Sea*, her writing never earned substantial sums. There was never a living in it for her until then.

Rescue came in the form of legacies received upon the decease of Tilden Smith's mother in 1934 and father in 1935. The Tilden Smiths went through their money fast. Still, as a couple they were never as poor as they had been at the time of their marriage. On 25 February 1936, after a short visit with Maryvonne in Holland, the Tilden Smiths sailed for the West Indies for the only return to Dominica of Rhys's life (Angier, 351). En route, they sailed through the Sargasso Sea.

Rhys was sorely disappointed with her old home. Things had changed or were not as she remembered. She visited the Lockhart family estate, Geneva, which had been burned down again a few years before her arrival. The tragic ruins were imprinted in her mind, and her creativity later would transform her imagining of the twentieth-century fire into the description of the nineteenth-century catastrophe in *Wide Sargasso Sea*. Dominica's legacy to its Creole child was to give her inspiration and material for her greatest novel.

The Tilden Smiths sailed home to England via New York, the art deco city that Rhys then found almost as exciting as Paris of the 1920s. But Rhys was now a violent alcoholic, abusive to her husband and given to uncontrollable rages. Writing provided the structure for her life, the moments of lucidity and sanity, but it was harder and harder for Rhys to put pen to paper. Out of the miasma of alcohol, anger, frustration, and despair came Rhys's darkest, most pessimistic novel, the tragic story of a middle-age woman falling, *Good Morning, Midnight,* published in 1939. It was Rhys's last book for twenty-five years. She did start a "Jane Eyre" novel, but despite the encouragement of Tilden Smith, she abandoned the project, or through drunkenness misplaced or lost what she had written.

At the beginning of World War II, Rhys was in London much of the time, while her husband, who was commissioned in the RAF in 1940, was on active duty at various base assignments in Britain (Angier, 373). When the Germans conquered Holland, Rhys lost touch with Maryvonne and was distraught and lonely. Fortunately, Maryvonne survived the war, as did her father. Both were involved in the Dutch Resistance. Meanwhile whenever the Tilden Smiths were together, the drunken wife embarrassed or humiliated the officer. Apparently Rhys's behavior, which included being arrested for drunkenness and being a public nuisance, forced Tilden Smith to resign his commission in October 1942 and take care of her in London (Angier, 425). He tried to make a living for them once more as a publisher's reader. Obtaining some money from relatives, the couple rented a remote cottage near Dartmoor, in which, on 2 October 1945, alone with Rhys, Tilden Smith, only sixty years old, died of a sudden heart attack (Angier, 428–29). Rhys was a solitary figure, feeling guilt for not having been a better partner and wife to the nurturing man who had been her second husband. But she was left with no money and had to resort to selling her deceased husband's books and other possessions for food and to pay the meager funeral expenses.

Literary Obscurity and Third Marriage

With her husband's sudden death, Rhys stopped writing entirely. He had probably provided the impetus for her short-story efforts in the war years. Exactly two years to the day after the death of Tilden Smith, on 2 October 1947, Jean Rhys married Max Hamer, a former World War I naval officer who had studied law after his 21 years of naval service and had become a solicitor (Angier, 440). During World War II, like Tilden Smith, he returned to military service as a training officer. Hamer was Tilden Smith's cousin and was helping Rhys with the estate. She was 57; he was 65. Hamer was another handsome, well-spoken English gentleman of good family background. A year before the marriage, Rhys and Hamer had begun living together in Hamer's house in Beckenham, a South London suburb.

Rhys had dropped out of the literary world. Her books were no longer in print. Because of her alcoholism and paranoia, she had lost all of her literary contacts and friends. Maryvonne had gone off to Indonesia with her husband and Rhys's granddaughter. The Hamers were very short of money and they fought over what they had. Max drank a lot, too, and had fallen in with some shady underworld characters. Troubles came in battalions. Rhys got into a brawl with a neighbor because of a dog and cat fight and was bound over to keep the peace. The Hamers rented out the top floor of their house, and Rhys subsequently fought with the tenants. She was arrested for assault, tried, found guilty, and fined in Bromley Magistrates Court (Angier, 444). At home she fought again with the tenants and was in and out of court so much that the magistrate questioned her sanity, and at the end of June 1948 she was sent to Holloway Prison Hospital for psychiatric observation. Released within a week, Rhys was sentenced to two years probation with the condition that she obtain appropriate psychiatric treatment (Angier, 447). She had been at war with her neighbors and tenants for a almost a year and a half.

In the midst of the conflicts and the trauma, someone had been searching for Rhys. The actress Selma vaz Dias advertised in the *New Statesman* in an attempt to locate the whereabouts of Jean Rhys in order to request permission to perform an adaptation of *Good Morning, Midnight* she had written for radio (Howells, 7). Vaz Dias did not know if Rhys was alive or dead, and no one else seemed to know either. The BBC thought Rhys had died in Paris years back. Selma had already planned a public performance even before she placed the advertisement. Rhys responded and she worked with vaz Dias on the script but did not attend the reading. She was in trouble again with the police. On 16 November 1949, she was arrested once more for being drunk and disorderly (Angier, 450). Fortunately, a different magistrate dismissed the charges. Rhys's behavior was now irrational. She fought again with two sets of tenants and was back in Bromley Court.

Then total disaster came: Hamer was arrested for larceny and obtaining money by false pretenses (Angier, 453). He had been led astray by a clever con man posing as his friend. The 68-year-old Hamer's judgment seems to have weakened. Hamer and Rhys raised bail by selling their furnishings. Unrelated to the legal problems, the BBC turned down a broadcast of *Good Morning, Midnight*. It was as if Nemesis had struck the elderly couple. During the trial, with Max free on bail, the Hamers moved into a cheap Kensington hotel room. On 22 May 1950 Hamer was convicted and sentenced to three years imprisonment (Angier, 457). He was released in two.

Meanwhile Rhys was totally alone. She stopped corresponding with vaz Dias and everyone else. In 1951 she moved to Maidstone, near where Hamer was incarcerated, and where she was treated as a drunken old lady living in cheap rented rooms (Angier, 459). Subsisting on meager family charity from people ashamed to associate with her, she visited her husband in prison and she tried to write. When Hamer was released in 1952, he and Rhys returned to London and settled in suburban rooms in Upper Norwood (Angier, 465). Max was 70. He was not eligible for an old-age pension because he had never contributed to the fund. He had lost his naval pension because he was a convicted felon. His health was destroyed. The couple lived in grinding poverty. Indeed, the existence of the Hamers for the rest of Max's life was hellish. They wandered about England, Cornwall, and Wales looking for an acceptable, affordable abode for their old age.

Trying to get her life together and perhaps earn some money, early in 1953 Rhys wrote to vaz Dias for help in restarting her writing career, but because the Hamers kept moving and never had a phone, contact was lost again (Angier, 465). The Hamers' judgment was clouded. They considered living in a small mobile home; they moved into the cabin on a moored yacht for a time; they were often cramped and bitterly cold in their various accommodations. After a hotel room in London for two years they moved to a holiday cottage in Bude, Cornwall (Angier, 468).

In the autumn of 1956, seven years after the first broadcast adaptation of *Good Morning, Midnight,* the BBC went looking for Rhys again. The next May vaz Dias wrote an article for the *Radio Times* implying that she had just found Jean Rhys and learned that the author was at work on a new novel (Angier, 472). In fact it was the interest of the BBC in her and their inviting her to London to attend rehearsals that stimulated Rhys into considering again the "Jane Eyre" work.

A Writer Again

Good Morning, Midnight was broadcast on 10 and 11 May 1957. The Hamers had to find a friend with a radio that could pick up the BBC Third Programme (Angier, 472). Rhys was very happy over the production and the attention she received. To her delight, the publisher André Deutsch offered her a small advance as an option on the novel she had just begun to work on again after many years. Rhys hoped the gestation period for the book, which would eventually be titled *Wide Sargasso Sea,* would be nine months. It took nine years.

Hamer's health continued to deteriorate (Angier, 480, 499). Slowly, but inevitably, Rhys, who had always expected men to take care of her, had to assume the full burden of caring for and then nursing her husband. She could have left him or allowed him to be taken to a nursing home, but she refused. She did her loyal duty to a stricken spouse. She was not always kind to Max, especially when his nursing needs interfered with the flow of her writing, but she did not abandon him. When he was very ill she could not write. When there was improvement there was time for writing. Short stories, old unpublished ones and new pieces, brought in money and, when in print, stimulated more interest in Rhys.

The Hamers started moving again. They chose abysmally. Finally and compassionately, if not generously, Rhys's brother Edward located and moved them to a small rundown cottage, No. 6 Landboat Bungalows, at the Devon village of Cheriton Fitzpaine (Angier, 482). It was barely adequate, but superior to most of the domiciles they had inhabited in their difficult marriage. The old cottage was the last real home for both Jean and Max. Of course Rhys got drunk often and in public, fought with her neighbors, and was paranoid, but somehow the people of the rural village were a little more accepting of the "crazy old lady with the invalid husband" than people in London and the suburbs. This was due in part to the kindness and understanding of the local Anglican rector, Alwynne Woodward, who almost alone of the villagers, knew that Rhys was a writer, although he probably had never read any of her work and may not have known about her earlier success. But perhaps because it was therapeutic and could assuage the rage in Rhys, he praised her writing, encouraged her, and kept her lubricated with just enough whiskey to keep her calm but still alert (Angier, 484–95).

Francis Wyndham, assigned as her editor at Deutsch, was also a true friend. Rhys had problems with the physical and mechanical aspects of preparing a novel-length manuscript. She could not type. She was forever misplacing pages and losing her continuity. Volunteer typing help, for which Rhys was never grateful, was found by Wyndham.

Hamer was dying. Rhys sometimes neglected him and even physically abused him as she had Tilden Smith, but she was doing such a dangerous thing: she was creating the character of a Creole mad woman, Antoinnette of *Wide Sargasso Sea,* and the creation was too close to her own psyche, to frighteningly like a prophecy of a potential future Rhys, the ghost of a Rhys yet to come. Simultaneously she must have thought or sensed that an old man was dying but a great novel was being given life. She knew good work when she saw it and when she wrote it. She was her own toughest, unsparing critic. By the spring of 1963, Hamer was regularly in and out of the hospital (Angier, 497). What seemed to hold the suffering old man to life was his deep, undying love for his wife. But each change was a trauma for Rhys. In April of the next year, Hamer was placed in a nursing home. Rhys was physically exhausted and ready for a breakdown.

Women came to Rhys's rescue. It was the sixties, and women were more conscious than ever before, and perhaps ever since, of their collective emotional needs, the necessity of mutual support in the masculinized work world, the political importance of sisterhood, and the responsibility they had to each other. The editor Diana Athill brought the young junior editor Esther Whitby down to Devon, along with typewriter, tape recorder, and writing supplies, to live with Rhys, type, edit, organize, and supply a support system.

But a woman also seems to have betrayed Rhys. Early in July of 1963 vaz Dias came for a visit with whiskey and a contract giving her half of the proceeds from any dramatic adaptations of Jean Rhys's work (Angier, 500). In the fog of alcohol Rhys signed, not fully realizing what she had done. Later she felt that vaz Dias had taken advantage of her friendship and condition, and was going to deprive Maryvonne and Rhys's granddaughter of money she wished them to have. But vaz Dias had been Rhys's rediscoverer and a supportive friend for some fourteen years. Of course, neither Rhys nor vaz Dias knew that there would also be movie money. Eventually, vaz Dias was persuaded to ease the financial terms of the contract to 30 percent of the dramatic proceeds (Angier, 638). Rhys and vaz Dias are both dead now, but their heirs are doing well out of Rhys's creative work.

Sonia Orwell, George Orwell's widow, became another supportive friend with literary appreciation and understanding, as Rosamond Lehmann had been much earlier. Orwell published parts of *Wide Sargasso Sea* in the January 1964 issue of *Art & Literature*, further whetting the reading public's and the publishing world's anticipation of the novel (Howells, 107). On 21 May 1964 the worn out, exhausted Rhys posted the completed novel to Deutsch (Angier, 517). Her masterpiece was done. Rhys was nearly 74.

Relieved of a nine-year monkey on the back and no longer driven by internal and external pressures, Rhys drank heavily, attacked a neighbor, collapsed, and was admitted to the Belvedere Clinic of Exe Vale Hospital near Exeter, where she remained one month (Angier, 518). In late

August 1964 Rhys returned home to the cottage at Cheriton Fitzpaine, but although she was rested she returned to heavy drinking. A few weeks later she had a heart attack, and Maryvonne was called from Holland, where she and her family were living since being driven out of Java by the Indonesian Revolution (Angier, 503, 519). Jean's friends came to visit and to help: Athill, Whitby, Rhys's cousin Lily Lockhart, and also vaz Dias, despite the strain in the relationship. Brother Edward also appeared and of course so did Francis Wyndham (Angier, 519–20).

After the hospital stay Rhys was in a series of nursing homes and actually lost contact with her friends for months because of her frequent moves caused by her constant dissatisfaction with her accommodations. Finally she came home to Cheriton Fitzpaine. Rhys had recovered but needed heart medication for the remainder of her life. In her paranoia Rhys imagined a conspiracy to embarrass her by publishing her book too soon, which she now felt needed more revisions. She did manage to get Deutsch to allow her to make changes in *Wide Sargasso Sea* that in fact did improve the final product (Angier, 519).

In February of 1966 she was awarded £300 a year for five years from the Royal Literary Fund (Angier, 522). Rhys needed the money badly, but she was more thrilled with the honor. Contiguous with the award, and perhaps because of it, Rhys finally felt that *Wide Sargasso Sea* was almost good enough to be published.

Having suffered terribly, Hamer died in the hospital on 2 March 1966 (Angier, 523). He was cremated in Exeter. Rhys was so ill herself, she had stopped visiting her husband, but she grieved deeply and felt utterly lonely despite the frequent presence of her friends and a copious correspondence. With Hamer's death she lost interest in revising *Wide Sargasso Sea*. It was as if the creation of the novel was tied to their life together. Death broke the bond to both the man and the book. In October 1966 *Wide Sargasso Sea* appeared to excellent reviews, and Rhys, the "rediscovered" artist, had the success, the fame, and the income that had eluded her in her first career as a writer (Angier, 576). It was very late. She was 76. But it was not too late. Her long life went on, and she continued to write for nine more years. In truth, with Max's death writing became her life.

In 1967 Rhys received the W. H. Smith Prize for 1966 and the Heinemann Award (Angier, 579). Deutsch began to reissue her earlier novels. Her works were translated into her beloved French and into German, Dutch, and other languages. The success of *Wide Sargasso Sea* brought Rhys many new friends, such as Antonia Fraser, and old acquaintances "found" her. The next year she published *Tigers Are Better-Looking,* her first short story collection since *The Left Bank* in 1927. She was tiny, frail, unable to do many physical things, and often ill with the diseases and infirmities of old age, but her mind remained clear, and she could still create even as she entered her eighties.

Feminism and Rhys's Legacy

The women's movement embraced Rhys even though she was not a feminist, for women saw in her work and in her life a cautionary tale of passive women manipulated, used, and abused by men, of female artists unappreciated by the masculinized world of publishing, and of how a lack of self-confidence and strength leads women to dependency and self-destruction. In Rhys it was alcohol that was both her weapon of self-destruction and her escape.

Now her oldest friends and relatives began to die off, including her brother Edward in 1970, who, almost alone of the family, had aided her in her times of need (Angier, 601). Rhys's third story collection, *Sleep It Off, Lady,* came out in 1974. Rhys had become relatively affluent, but she continued to stay on in the cottage in Cheriton Fitzpaine, although sometimes wintering in London, because it was familiar and she knew she could work there. Young women who were her admirers continued to come into her life and make it more comfortable by improving the cottage.

The American writer David Plante appeared on the scene in 1974 to help Rhys with her stories and autobiography (Plante, 9–10). That same year she received a Civil List pension for life in recognition of her service to literature (Angier, 605). In February 1976 Rhys fell and broke several ribs (Angier, 629). After a stay in a nursing home she returned to Cheriton Fitzpaine, where her friends arranged for a nurse and a housekeeper to look after her. Rhys's last completed book, the end of her significant fiction, *Sleep It Off, Lady,* was published in October of that year.

In 1977 Rhys received a substantial Arts Council Award to write her autobiography. In 1978 Rhys received the highest government honor she would get, a C.B.E. (Commander, Order of the British Empire).

Early in 1977 Rhys and two young woman friends valiantly, almost insanely, set off on Rhys's last trip to the Continent, not to her beloved Paris as one might expect, but to Venice, which was a more manageable place for an old, bent, crippled woman, and of which Rhys had often dreamed of visiting (Angier, 635–36). It is not an exaggeration to say that the old lady had the time of her life, drinking champagne, pushed along the canals in her wheelchair, and riding in state in a gondola. Then it was back to Cheriton Fitzpaine. Now, in 1977, Rhys's sister, Brenda, her bitter sibling rival, died (Angier, 639). Rhys was now the last of the Williams's children alive.

Rhys had been spending her winters in London in different hotels, never satisfied with any. Her last London abode was not a hotel but the home of one of her supporters, the generous Di Melly (Angier, 643). Melly waited on Rhys hand and foot, giving the writer precedence over her husband and children, but after three months she was close to a breakdown herself from Rhys's ungrateful, difficult, demanding ways and her unpredictable personality shifts between rage and depression. Even Maryvonne and Rhys's granddaughter, Ellen, were treated rudely, perhaps cruelly when they visited. Finally Rhys was returned to Cheriton Fitzpaine, leaving a wake of stunned, exhausted, and embittered friends (Angier, 647). Rhys's last battle with friends and supporters, and all who cared for and about her, was her endgame with death. For all her misery and misfortune, she loved life, perhaps in her affluent and powerful old age even more than in her youth. Death would not manipulate, use, and betray her as long as she had breath and strength to hold it off.

Rhys refused to stay in a nursing home when, in 1978, after recuperating from a fall, it was clearly the best thing for her to do (Angier, 649). She was 88 and bent like a bow. She finished the first part of the autobiography, *Smile Please*, a painful work she had really been unwilling to undertake in her extreme old age, but one that she pursued because she felt angry about what some writers had said of her, and she wished to state the facts of her life as she recalled them.[7] The publishers decided to publish it in two parts, perhaps realizing that the autobiography would never be completed.

Early in 1979 a rest in a nursing home helped a little. She was skeletal when she again returned to her cottage. In April she fractured her hip in a fall and had to go to the hospital (Angier, 652). Before her fall she was still signing contracts for the publication of stories and giving interviews. During her three weeks in the Royal Devon and Exeter Hospital, Rhys faded away. She died on 14 May 1979, almost alone but for a friend, Jo Batterham, who happened to be passing through, and who had stopped off to see Rhys (Angier, 653). Her life, so full of pain and rage, came to darkness quietly, like a window shade slowly drawn down. A woman held her hand.

Chapter Two

The Left Bank and Other Stories

Rhys's first book, *The Left Bank and Other Stories,* is a collection of stories, published with an extraordinary self-serving preface by Ford Madox Ford, an egregious act of gender imperialism more than 20 pages long, with only 5 about Rhys. There is no story in the collection titled "The Left Bank"; that is really the title of Ford's preface: "Rive Gauche." Rhys's work is the 22 pieces that constitute the "Other." Perhaps the book should have been called *Other Stories.* Indeed, much of the collection is not set on the Left Bank; that is, the XIIIth arrondissement of Paris, the boulevard du Montparnasse area, with its cafés and expatriate writers and artists such as Hemingway, Stein, and Picasso.

Ford seems to have tried to steer his disciple toward a more precise geography, but Rhys already had an ear for economy in writing and perhaps an unconscious understanding of the correctness of generalizing her experiences. In his preface Ford says he made an effort to "induce the author of *The Left Bank* to introduce some sort of topography of the region . . . into her sketches" (*LB,* 25–26). But when he called her attention to the matter, Rhys, from the beginning her own person as a writer, "eliminated even such two or three words of descriptive matter as had crept into her work. Her business was with passion, hardship, emotions: the locality in which these things are endured is immaterial" (*LB,* 26).

But there is a spirit in *The Left Bank* that is both Rhys's and that of the area and the milieu, and it is not only in the Paris stories where it has been observed that "the Paris ambiance is suffused through nearly every page."[1] The Rhys-Parisian spirit is in the longest and finest tale, "Vienne," set in Vienna, Budapest, and Prague, and even in the pieces located on the Riviera or in the West Indies. With a unique, woman's perspective, that of the outsider on the fringe of a Bohemia, the underworld, and a baffling Continental culture, Rhys, the beginner, produced the type of tough, unsentimental narratives and observations, with stark characters foregrounded against a dark mood, that would remain her trademark.

Paris Stories

The *Left Bank* begins with a powerful but subtle story, "Illusion," which introduces Rhys's theme of women watching other women and finding them complicated and deep in ways that male writers might not perceive. A prim and proper English woman living in Paris, Miss Bruce, a mediocre artist with a private income, is stricken with appendicitis and sent to the hospital. She appears to be a conservative woman who dresses sensibly and who seems untouched "after seven years in Paris" by anything unwholesome or exotic in the city that epitomized "the cult of beauty and the worship of physical love" (*LB*, 29).

When on the request of the landlady, the narrator, Miss Bruce's friend of slight acquaintance, goes to the artist's room to collect some items from the wardrobe for the ill woman's hospital stay, she finds a plethora of chic designer clothes, as well as expensive perfumes and jewels. Appearance is not reality. Miss Bruce is not what she seems. The implication is that Miss Bruce wears the clothes in private, and even she hungers to be beautiful and to be loved.

When Miss Bruce meets the narrator after the hospital stay, she denies that she ever wears the exotic clothes. It is only a collection, she says, as she attempts to save her "illusion." So, like Colette, Rhys knows the fears and the pressures that motivate women to repress and hide their dreams not only from other women but from themselves. Yet there is a final twist to the story. When dining with the narrator weeks after returning from the hospital, Miss Bruce admires a girl who is gazing into the eyes of her escort. " 'Not bad hands and arms, that girl!' said Miss Bruce in her gentlemanly manner" (*LB*, 36). The story concludes with the words "gentlemanly manner," and the reader is forced to stop and ask what does that mean in relation to the character that Rhys has created, and are there not several "meanings" possible—a purposeful ambiguity? how does this final episode of the story relate to the central one: the discovery of the finery?

Now Miss Bruce is observing another woman and in doing so causes the reader to rethink Miss Bruce and her clothes. Is Rhys ever so subtly hinting at "closet" lesbianism? Do the clothes stand in for bodies, the perfumes for the longed-for scent of another woman? Rhys is a clever storyteller, who with great modernist economy gives the reader just enough information to require him or her to come to a personal conclusion, to fill out and complete the narrative. The reader may supply the

ending of the tale by pronouncing a verdict from the ambiguous, circumstantial evidence or choose to leave the case open.

Reflecting Rhys's experience in Paris as a clothes model, "Mannequin" is a sharply focused story that brings us behind the scene in the
fashion world, where working for a couturier is exposed as far from
glamorous. Anna, a beautiful young model just starting a career and a
job, is full of romantic expectations. In the "mannequins' dressing-room
she spent a shy hour making up her face—in an extraordinary and distinctive atmosphere of slimness and beauty; white arms and faces vivid
with rouge; raucous voices and the smell of cosmetics; silken lingerie"
(*LB*, 60–61). But the reality of the place is seen in the room itself: "a
depressing room, taken by itself, bare and cold, a very inadequate con-
servatory for these human flowers" (*LB*, 61).

The other girls are not very friendly. Madame Pecarde, the dresser,
who is kind to Anna, is disparaged by the others. The women are
treated like furniture by salespeople and buyers. In reality Anna is only
another exploited worker in a fiercely competitive industry. The work is
hard, the day very long. Yet at the end the young woman deludes herself
in feeling that "now she really belonged to the great" (*LB*, 69). Out on
the rue de la Paix, "the maddening city possessed her and she was
happy" (*LB, 69*).

"Tea with an Artist" presents a painter, presumably described by the
same persona who revealed Miss Bruce. The artist Verhausen, who is
Flemish and not given a first name, apparently is gifted, but he refuses,
rather perversely, to either exhibit or sell his paintings. His first wife,
wanting money, did manage to sell some before she left him, and he
knows that after he is dead his second wife, a former prostitute with the
sensibilities and values of an uneducated peasant, will sell or perhaps
destroy all the rest. But the couple are happy. He is his own person,
independent of the bourgeois world of buying and selling, and the wife
has accepted a role the narrator envies but presumably cannot replicate.
The wife's "business in life had been the consoling of men" (*LB*, 81).

In this story Rhys indicates an understanding of the retentiveness of
the artist. The perspective is feminine. The works are the children and
they need more care and nurturing. Rhys seems to be foreshadowing her
own reluctance later to let go of her novels so that they could be published.

In the story "In the Rue de l'Arrivée" the protagonist, Dolly
Dufreyne, is the prototype of "the faded woman" with "the clear look of
youth going—gone" (*LB*, 115), who was to become the typical Rhys

heroine in her later novels (Howells, 33). She is an alcoholic, heavily drinking to hide from herself the depths to which she has sunk. She was "down on her luck . . . and was doomed to the fate of the feeble who have not found a protector" (*LB*, 114). As she staggers home, a man tries to pick her up and she insults him. To her surprise he does not insult her back. Instead he mutters a sympathetic remark and passes on. Later Dolly realizes that "only the hopeless are starkly sincere and that only the unhappy can either give or take sympathy" (*LB*, 120–21). Even bitter misery has its strange voluptuousness, and an angel may be "dressed in a shabby suit" although, paradoxically, he may take one to hell (*LB*, 121).

In "A Spiritualist" the narrator, a military or police "commandant," cannot understand why his deceased mistress was so unhappy with him that her ghost tries to do him violence. After all, he states, "I adore women—that without a woman in my life I cannot exist" (*LB*, 37). But she, who had been a young dancer, has been used, exploited, and controlled by him, and in death he has neglected to get her the white marble tombstone he promised, so her ghost throws a chunk of marble at him, but, unfortunately, misses. Rhys had plenty of experience already with that kind of man, and if then she still repressed her desire to do violence to those smug controllers, she at least could express her fury in words and, atypically for her, assuage her anger with humor.

"In a Café" is a slice-of-life vignette set in a Parisian café in the "Quarter," patronized by prostitutes and their customers. An entertainer sings a sentimental song about the "*grues*," the prostitutes. They "are the sellers of illusion of Paris, the frail and sometimes pretty ladies" (*LB*, 51). Everyone in the café is moved: "All the women there looked into their mirrors during the progress of the song: most of them rouged their lips. The men stopped reading their newspapers, drank up their beers thirstily and looked sideways" (*LB*, 52). Rhys is sympathetic with the women as they check their faces and cover up the signs of aging and imperfection, while the men glance around guiltily to see if other men are moved too.

In a further vignette, "In the Luxembourg Gardens," a depressed young man meets a young woman for the first time, and life has meaning for him once more. The narrator in "Tout Montparnasse and a Lady" mocks an artificial lemonade-drinking American fashion artist, a supercilious woman who has come into one of the watering holes of the Anglo-Saxon expatriate community to observe and look down on the patrons. One man, whom she has been gazing at reprovingly, says "Oh

God! How I hate women who write! How I *hate* them!" (*LB*, 56). Soon
she finds herself attracted to a young man whom she thinks is a "dope
fiend," only to learn that he is a respectable artist. When, however, she
makes up to him, he puts her down with indignation. Rhys, on the other
hand, puts the whole scene down as a pastiche of Chelsea (London),
Greenwich Village, Moscow, and other Bohemian abodes.

In the stream-of-conciousness monologue "Hunger," a woman lying
in a hotel room depicts the suffering and depression stemming from
being broke and not having anything to eat for five days. "The acceptance of her condition and the ironic rendering of her fate . . . anticipate
in an embryonic way the characteristics and attitudes of the female character which is to develop in later novels" (Staley, 29).

"Discourse of a Lady Standing a Dinner to a Down-and-Out Friend"
continues the narrative of the destitute persona in the texts. Here, in a
monologue and asides, a well-off woman castigates her hungry and
impoverished friend for not handling her life better and taking more
care of her appearance, even though she knows the friend is desperately
in need of financial help. The speaker enjoys lording it over her poor
friend, and the reader joins the friend in hating the cruel condescension.
The fine meal costs too much in pride and feeling.

In "In a Night" the character is so miserably lonely that she prays for
company. The persona in "In Learning to Be a Mother" gives birth in
sordid surroundings, a midwife's factory or barn of suffering and indif-
ference, and what she learns amid the screams of women in agony, and
after her own have ceased, is that she loves her son despite the suffering
he has caused her.

The mini short story "The Blue Bird" has the narrator observe the life
of a woman addicted to bad men who use and betray her. When one,
wanted by the police, kills himself, the woman laments not having died
with her lover and promptly finds herself another "bad man" (*LB,* 140).
This blue bird finds happiness, perversely, in her unhappiness. In "The
Grey Day" a young man finds it hard to be creative in the dreary
cityscape and in his impoverished environs, even if it is Paris.

Prison Stories

Two of Rhys's Paris stories in *The Left Bank* are set in a prison, where
Lenglet was incarcerated and where Rhys went to visit him. In "From a
French Prison" the narrator describes the queue of visitors waiting to see
their loved ones. Most are women, "the sort that trouble had whipped

into a becoming meekness" (*LB*, 44). Rhys often insists that trouble breaks women and in making them meek makes them attractive to men. For her everyone is a prisoner of the system and society. The warder acts like "some petty god." Rhys must have experienced the insolence of petty office every time she waited outside and then in line to see her jailed husband for a few minutes once a week.

In the story the prisoners strain to catch sight of their visitors and rush to talk for the mere 15 minutes allowed. The focus of pity is not on a prisoner but on a poor old man, a visitor so confused by the procedures that in the end he breaks down and cries. It is much more effective, more interesting, more objective to shift the feeling away from the criminals to the victims of love.

"The Sidi" is a Moroccan prisoner, young and "beautiful as some savage Christ" (*LB*, 148), a religious Muslim who speaks very little French. His chants fill the prison with pleasing exotic sound as if he is singing to Allah, but all he can ask for from his fellow prisoners is tobacco. Taken ill before his trial, he cannot inform a brutal jailer that he is sick, and he is heartlessly clubbed to death. In this existential universe humans cannot communicate with each other through the bars, either by words or by tapping or by understanding. Opportunities to help our fellow humans are few and far between. When lost they are regretted.

West Indies Stories

Two stories in *The Left Bank* are set in the Antilles, prefigured by the very short "Trio," in which the narrator observes a black family eating. The man is dressed in a lounge suit, but the woman wears "the native Martinique turban, making no pretensions to fashion. Her bodice and skirt gaped apart and through the opening a coarse white cotton chemise peeped innocently forth. . . . From the Antilles" (*LB*, 84). The happy child with the couple gets up to sing and dance. She is applauded by her father but admonished by her mother to "keep yourself quiet" (*LB*, 85), and the narrator knows that "it was because these were my compatriots that in that Montparnasse restaurant I remembered the Antilles" (*LB*, 85). Thus Rhys's secret background is insinuated in the text. She remembers her own childhood, and she knows that the pretty girl is born to perform for the pleasure of men, but she must not express herself wildly, indecorously, or make too much of a stir.

In "Mixing Cocktails," the persona is a child again, back in Dominica, remembering warm tropical days in a stream-of-consciousness monologue. Her life is full of limitations and restrictions. Her mother recites a litany of her "bad" habits. English visitors condescend. Her father is busy. The sun will give her freckles. The cook, Ann Twist, an "old obeah (Voodoo) woman," warns "you all must'n look too much at de moon" (LB, 91). The implication is that the moon will drive her mad, but of course to want to look at the moon is to seek romance and to aspire. But all that the narrator is socially conditioned to do, as a dominant culture white hostess to be, is to "mix cocktails very well and swizzle them better" (LB, 91). Pitifully, she remarks "here is something I can do," and she ironically concludes "action, they say, is more worthy than dreaming" (LB, 92).

"Again the Antilles" humorously relates a little culture war between the "coloured" editor of a Dominican newspaper and a white landowner. Discourse is the battleground as the landowner writes letters to the editor and he responds. Of course the dominant discourse is that of the colonizer, the Englishman; and Papa Dom, the editor, who has tried to assimilate and sound English, is at a disadvantage when in quoting he mistakes Chaucer for Shakespeare. The landowner is triumphant, stating "it is indeed a saddening and a dismal thing that the names of great Englishmen should be thus taken in vain by the ignorant of another race and colour" (LB, 96). Of course the statement is code for racism. He had really written "damn niggers," but the editor had edited it out. His rejoinder is to take the landowner to task for not being an English gentleman regardless of the fact that he misplaced Chaucer's "very gentle, perfect knight." But the editor can't win, of course, for the dominant discourse enshrines "the values of one particular culture as axiomatic, as literary or textual givens."[2]

Riviera Stories

Two stories in the collection are set on the Riviera. "At the Villa d'Or" a young Jewish woman named Sara works for a fabulously wealthy American couple whose villa on the Mediterranean "might have been the Villa of the Golden Calf" (LB, 155). The Americans are superficial and indolent. Riviera life maintains perverted values; singers must work as gardeners and fine artists as decorators or painters of flattering portraits of the rich in order to survive while pursuing their art. Yet Sara is very happy there, for "in Paris one was fear-haunted, insecure, one caught terrifying glimpses of the Depths and the monsters who live there. . . . At the Villa d'Or life was something shallow . . . that tinkled meaninglessly . . . shallow but safe" (*LB*, 159). Rhys herself had found, in her brief sojourn on the Riviera in 1926 as a ghostwriter for a rich American woman, some respite from her trials in Paris.

"La Grosse Fifi" is the second longest story in *The Left Bank*, exceeded in length only by the last story, "Vienne." In contrast to the Villa d'Or, a seedy hotel is the setting for this story of the exploitation, abuse, and finally murder of a woman made vulnerable by the masochistic power of romantic fantasy. Ford had required Rhys to read the short stories of Guy de Maupassant. The title "La Grosse Fifi" is reminiscent of the title of an 1882 Maupassant story, "Mademoiselle Fifi," a story of a courageous prostitute in the Franco-Prussian War who strikes a blow for her country against the German invaders.

Rhys's narrator is a girl named Roseau, the name of Rhys's home town in Dominica, surely chosen so that the author could code her identification with the character. "Roseau" is French for reed, and this may symbolize Rhys's perception of herself as a weak, slender, easily breakable plant.

Fifi is an aging, overweight woman who will do anything for her young gigolo. She is kindhearted and befriends Roseau, who has just lost her man. Roseau witnesses the humiliation, self-abasement, and mistreatment that leads to the death of her older friend at the hands of her gigolo, and she sees in that vicarious and cautionary experience the destiny she must flee, so as the story ends, "she dried her eyes and went on with her packing" (*LB*, 191). Arnold E. Davidson notes that the youthful Rhys creates in "La Grosse Fifi" a "character who reads in an older other woman something of what her own fate will probably be."[3]

"Vienne"

The last and longest story in *The Left Bank*, "Vienne," was first published in the *Transatlantic Review* in a shorter, three-sketch version. It seems that *The Left Bank* version of "Vienne," because of its considerable plot, numerous interesting characters about whom we would like to know more, varied locales, and large quantities of suspense and tension, was an intermediary and preparatory piece for a novel, one, of course, that was either never written or never published. "Vienne" is the story of a young married couple—Francine, an English woman (the narrator), and Pierre, a Frenchman—who, in the chaos after the end of World War I, have come to Vienna, where Pierre has a job as an advisor and interpreter for Colonel Ishima, a member of the Japanese delegation to a commission of Allied officers involved in the occupation of Vienna, the conquered capital of the former Austro-Hungarian Empire.

The story is a reminiscence, told in short, titled scenes, as if a photograph album was given headings. The narrator says "Funny how it's slipped away, Vienna. Nothing left but a few snapshots" (LB, 193). But it hasn't slipped away. The photographs merge into a clear picture of a relationship, an adventure, and a milieu. Francine sees the actions of her life and their consequences all too clearly. The young couple live a riotous life of cabarets, night clubs, and luxury hotels (such as the famous Sacher) on the illicit money Pierre obtains through currency manipulation. But from the beginning the story foreshadows disaster.

Francine loves the money: "Oh, great god money—you make possible all that's nice in life. Youth and beauty, the envy of women, and the love of men" (LB, 221–22). Initially, Francine is content to observe the sad lives of young women of the demimonde, who are little more than war booty, as they "learn to accept the most brutal rebuffs with a smile and keep one's dignity" (LB, 227). The narrator satirizes the Japanese employers of her husband for their rapaciousness, but their lasciviousness is not because they are Japanese but because they are men in power, who have total control of their wives and geishas at home in Japan and of the secretaries and entertainers they use in Vienna.

Pierre's commission is transferred to the second former capital of the Austro-Hungarian Empire, Budapest, where tragedy hits home and Francine loses the luxury of being the observer, becoming the victim of her husband's cupidity and criminality. Pierre is a controlling, manipulative, clever, amoral man who considers himself more intelligent than those he works for and with. As a result, using his employers' money, he has participated in currency fraud and manipulation. Now, in Budapest, he believes he has been betrayed by one of the Japanese officers he has worked for. Terrified and without courage, he plans suicide. Francine drags the truth out of her husband, abandons her passivity, talks Pierre out of self-destruction, and helps formulate a plan to escape. She says, "Let's go, let's get away . . . and shut up about killing yourself. If you kill yourself you know what will happen to me?" (LB, 240). The escape adventure across borders begins, although from the beginning Francine plans to go to London to borrow money.

Driven by their chauffeur in their expensive limousine, they crash through the Czechoslovak border and wind up in Prague, where after dismissing their driver they take one last ride alone in their already sold car and contemplate an Ethan Frome–like suicide by smashing into a tree. But they are too full of the love of life to die young. Pierre wants to go to Warsaw, but for Francine, "it was: 'Nach London' " (*LB*, 256). It is not clear in these last words of the text if Pierre will go with Francine, but at last she is in control of her own life, and salvation is in the city from where she has come to the Continent.

One reason for the significance of "Vienne" is that the story illustrates a plot pattern that was more fully developed in Rhys's work later, in which the heroine is at first entrapped in emotional and material dependency, a victim of the fantasies of youth and love, and then manages to overcome these impediments and both accepts and takes charge of her own destiny. "Vienne" reads like a lyrical, dramatic dialogue with limited description, a relationship played out in passion and high drama. It is a woman's narrative of coming to know the limitations of the man she loves and depends upon and of achieving the realization that her life is really her own.

The Left Bank was a remarkable beginning for Rhys. For the contemporary reader, these early stories helped specify "this author's vision of her world" (Davidson, 113). Her mentor, Ford, surely saw her ability and great potential. It is to his credit that he published her first work and encouraged her to pursue the narrative art.

Chapter Three
Quartet

Quartet, originally published as *Postures*, is Jean Rhys's fictionalized version of the ménage à trois in Paris that Ford Madox Ford and Stella Bowen conned her into. It is also her revenge on Ford and Bowen, and it is her exorcism of what was perhaps the most terrible episode of sexual exploitation, masculine betrayal, and emotional manipulation in her life. Critical reception was more negative than positive, with reviewers in Britain and America objecting to the author's depiction of a shockingly dissipated Parisian world yet recognizing the power of the writing (*Angier*, 178, 691).

Rhys's heroine Marya Zelli is a 28-year-old English woman who, like the central female persona in *The Left Bank*, is living on the edge of respectability and survival. Her husband, Stephan, a handsome and charming Pole a few years older that Marya and a dealer in stolen art work and antiques, falls into the hands of the police, leaving Marya alone and without funds.

Marya is a passive, dependent person, very susceptible to strong-minded "friends" who are determined to "help" her, namely H. J. and Lois Heidler (Germanic-sounding name, like Ford's original, Heuffer). *Quartet* is the sparse, concentrated tale of a woman's fall. From the time Marya feels Heidler's "hand lying heavily on her knee,"[1] under a table, the reader realizes that Marya is doomed to seduction and betrayal. The pressure of his hand on her knee will be replaced by the pressure of his gross body on hers as well as the pressure exerted by his money, his clever manipulations, and his male power.

But the narrator also symbolizes Marya's doom as resulting from the temptations of Parisian Bohemian life. Early in the text, at a bar, an ironically "fresh-faced boy" offers Marya a capsule guaranteed immediately to pull someone together who has been drinking too much: " 'Would you like to try one?' . . . He handed her over a small capsule. 'Break it, sniff it up, that's right.' Marya broke the capsule and inhaled. Her heart stopped with a jerk, then seemed to dilate suddenly and very painfully. The blood rushed over her face and neck. 'I'm going to fall,' she thought with terror, and clutched the edge of the table" (*Q*, 42). She does not insist on knowing the content of the drug capsule; she does not ask what it will do to her; she does not realize that evil may wear a "fresh face." Innocent, trusting, and naive, she does not consider the ultimate consequence of her actions.

The Heidlers: Portrait of a Marriage

Hugh J. Heidler, an art dealer, and his wife, Lois, a painter, have an arrangement in their marriage allowing Heidler to have young, impoverished mistresses living with them. Lois sees this as a way of keeping possession of this powerful man with a harem complex. She pretends to care for each "ward," like Marya, but really hates each young favorite and cannot wait for her to be thrown over by Heidler when he tires of her. Meanwhile Marya is the biscuit with which Lois keeps Heidler reasonably content on his loose leash. Later, when Marya is living with the Heidlers, feeling suspicious of them and wishing to leave, Lois, looking at Marya, thinks, "Oh, no, my girl, you won't go away. You'll stay here where I can keep an eye on you. It won't last long . . . It can't last long. I've always let him alone and given him what he wanted and it's never failed me. It won't fail me now. He'll get tired of her as soon as she gives in" (Q, 81).

Lois will do anything to keep her position as a married woman. Young, attractive women are her mortal enemies, who must be defeated by a mock surrender, pretended affection, and control. She exercises control over Marya by being hypocritically solicitous of Marya's poor health and difficult situation, promising help in finding a mannequin's job later and giving Heidler easy access to his prey. Lois nevertheless seems to get a certain sadomasochistic sexual pleasure out of the situation. She enjoys the humiliation of her husband's "love" for a younger, more attractive woman, his mental abuse of her, and the inevitable victory she will win over her rival. She shifts the focus for her understandable anger at her husband onto the young woman involved, in this case Marya. In other words, through marriage she appropriates some of her husband's patriarchal power, which, like a prison trustee, she can wield against other women.

Above all the Heidlers must keep up appearances, although everyone in their acquaintance knows what a goat he is, pretends pity for "poor" Lois, and despises the young woman they see as a home breaker. It is all good gossip for the community of Anglo-American expatriates. Rhys is saying that a bourgeois marriage like the Heidlers's is a sham. The respectable veneer-thin surface hides corruption, cruel manipulation, sadism, and masochism: the male with his balloon ego and rapacious lust never satisfied, the woman enduring anything to stay within the system. Although there is not much humor in the novel, the narrator and Marya are at least able to laugh at Heidler's hypocrisy. When Heidler lectures her that she has "got to play the game" of respectability (Q, 113), Marya thinks, "He looks exactly like a picture of Queen Victoria" (Q, 114). Of course Heidler makes the rules of this "game," one invented in Victorian times or earlier.

Heidler is extremely convincing in his seduction arguments. After all, he is well practiced, a professional, and his victims are amateurs. He has control of language. Indeed, Rhys implies that men always have control of language. It is one source of their power. Heidler claims that all he wants to do is make Marya happy and he will do it in spite of her (Q, 77).

Zelli is also capable of control through "logical" argument, as when he castigates Marya for leaving the Heidlers: "What do you want to be free for? . . . Really you must be mad to do a thing like that" [Q, 109]), and when he makes her feel guilty for missing a visit to him in prison (Q, 109). At the time Zelli was first courting Marya, he quickly took control of their relational discourse: "he criticized her clothes with authority and this enchanted her. He told her that her arms were too thin, that she had a Slav type and a pretty silhouette, that if she were happy and petted she would become charming. Happy, petted, charming—these are magical words" (Q, 18).

Marya has no cultural platform or traditional moral position to argue from. Although she has books to read and enjoys reading, she has no guiding texts, religious, traditional, or literary, to refer to, employ, or to lean on. She can complain of her suffering and express dislike and confusion, but she cannot say "this is wrong" and be listened to, understood, or believed, perhaps even by herself. When Stephan brings home an item he is going to fence, she is suspicious but cannot come out and condemn his actions, choosing only to question the legality of the provider's possession and then accepting Stephan's abrupt and sharp closing of the subject (Q, 21). When later she visits him in prison, she does not seem to understand that he has committed a wrongful act. Their trouble has been caused by "rotten luck" (Q, 36). In these ways the vulnerable Marya is an accesory in the cruelties and crimes that seal her fate.

"Good Samaritans"

Rhys chose a sardonic epigram for *Quartet:*

> Beware
> Of Good Samaritans—walk to the right
> Or hide thee by the roadside out of sight
> Or greet them with the smile that villains wear.
>   R. C. Dunning

Rhys would trust no one. The world of her fiction is a jungle of predators feeding on the naive, the helpless, the confused, and the lost. "Good Samaritans" like the Heidlers are motivated not out of charity or love of fellow humans but only by their own selfish desires. Walk away from or hide from the "Good Samaritans" says Rhys; or give them a measure of their own duplicity. Play villain yourself is her harsh, rather Brechtian advice, and you'll survive.

Marya, whom Stephan has left without funds, reluctantly agrees to move into the spidery trap that is the Heidler home, and she is prevented from leaving by the refusal of her host and hostess to lend her enough money so that she can afford a small place of her own. They wish to control her body, mind, and soul. Rhys symbolizes the relationship when she describes how they travel in a cab: "Marya sat squeezed between the Heidlers" (Q, 98). She comes between them, and she binds them together in the common purpose of preventing her escape until they are finished with her. When she is finally seduced, she falls in love with Heidler, her Svengali, and when he finally drops her, she is heartbroken.

The Heidlers have tried to keep her from visiting Stephan in prison, but out of pity and remembering her former love for her husband, she continues to visit him. She moves out of the Heidler home, but she allows Heidler, her controller, to set her up in a cheap hotel as his kept woman. There she has nothing to do but wait for his brief visits and carnal thrusting. She is alone and friendless; her job is sex; her life is waiting. As to the lovemaking,

> He wasn't a good lover, of course. He didn't really like women. She had known that as soon as he touched her. His hands were inexpert, clumsy at caresses; his mouth was hard when he kissed. No, not a lover of women, he could say what he liked. He despised love. He thought of it grossly, to amuse himself, and then with ferocious contempt. (Q, 118)

Sex for Heidler is "a ferocious thing . . . a terrible thing" (Q, 130). Not surprisingly Marya quickly grows depressed and falls ill. Her sense of torpor renders her continually more helpless as she comes to fully understand the powerlessness of her situation.

Cairn, a young, penniless, sentimental American man, an impecunious writer, tries to help the confused Marya to escape the Heidlers, when she confides, "I don't like him or trust him. I love him. D'you get me? And Lois says that she doesn't mind a bit and gives us her blessing—the importance of sex being vastly exaggerated . . . but she says that I mustn't give her away. So does Heidler. They call that playing the game" (Q, 93). But Cairn really cannot help her. She needs a protector with some money, and although they make a date to see each other again, she thinks, "there he was, incapable of helping. Before she had walked three steps from the Closerie des Lilas she had forgotten all about him" (Q, 94–95).

Rhys implies that in the context of early twentieth-century European society, a man is really only useful to Marya, and perhaps to any woman, when he can undertake an economic obligation to her and participate in the slave contract for the exchange of love, sex, and respect for male financial support, which, of course, eventually grows burdensome as the man realizes the woman is a parasite.

Regardless, it is too late. Exerting pressure, Heidler says, "I don't want you to see Cairn again," and Marya replies, "All right" (Q, 95). She is his broken creature, desiring only peace: "Peace had ascended on her and to that peace she was ready to sacrifice Cairn or anybody or anything" (Q, 95). Neither Cairn nor Stephan without money can provide peace, no matter how well meaning they are as friends, or good as lovers. Money is power in Rhys's work, total power. The few women who have it are or become insufferable to other women. The men who have money use it to control the Others: women, the poor, their children, Blacks, and servants.

Marya believes she loves Heidler, "but of course it wasn't a love affair. It was a fight. A ruthless merciless, three-cornered fight. And from the first Marya, as was right and proper, had no chance of victory. For she fought wildly, with tears, with futile rages, with extravagant abandon—all bad weapons" (Q, 117). A woman's traditional weapons are no defense against the patriarchal power of the Heidler marriage front. Eventually Marya understands and says to Heidler, "You've smashed me up, you two" (Q, 129). They have also made a child of her, an abused child. The Heidlers talk about dressing Marya in front of her: " 'She must be chic,' his wife went on. 'She must do us credit.' She might have been discussing the dressing of a doll" (Q, 85). Lois has Marya run errands for her. Stephan, too, has treated her like a child, not telling her the truth about his "work," never consulting her in planning for them, and giving love but requiring obedience. Significantly, both Zelli and the Heidlers call her by a pet name: "Mado." Heidler has also stripped Marya of the comfort and support of her religious faith. In a church Marya watches the hypocritical Heidler "go down on one knee and cross himself as he passed the altar. He glanced quickly sideways at her as he did it, and she thought: 'I'll never be able to pray again now that I've seen him do that. Never! However sad I am.' And she felt very desolate" (Q, 95). Perhaps she understands her loss of faith better when later she day dreams and sees Heidler kneeling again in the church and "looking sideways at her to see if she were impressed" (Q, 161). God or at least Heidler's version of God must be a white male. Heidler says, "God's a pal of mine. . . . He probably looks rather like me, with cold eyes and fattish hands. I'm in His image or He's in mine. It's all one. I prayed to Him to get you and I got you. Shall I give you a letter of introduction?" (Q, 161). Subtextually, Heidler is Marya's god, but he is neither loving nor forgiving. But, at least in her unconscious mind Marya can see through Heidler's "posturing, classifying, and rationalizing."[2]

Second Betrayal

When Stephan is released, Marya tries to begin life anew with him. The Heidlers finally meet Stephan and are contemptuous and patronizing. Marya, now fully disgusted with the Heidlers, returns to Stephan in their hotel room but unwisely informs him of the affair with Heidler, reminding Stephan that he had urged her to stay with the seemingly generous and good-hearted couple. Stephan, with typical male jealousy, anger, and furor, threatens to kill Heidler. When Marya tries to prevent him from leaving their hotel room to carry out his assault, he throws her down and leaves her unconscious after her head strikes the corner of a table.

Instead of going after Heidler he runs away with the prostitute companion of one of his jail mates. Having done violence to his wife, his sexual jealousy of his male rival appears abated. He is off with another woman while his wife lies unconscious and possibly dead in a squalid hotel room. Stephan thinks, "Encore *une grue*," for "at that moment women seemed to him loathsome, horrible—soft and disgusting weights suspended round the necks of men, dragging them downwards.

At the same time he longed to lay his head on Mademoiselle Chardin's shoulder and weep his life away" (*Q*, 186). Mademoiselle Chardin is only another prostitute to him, like his wife, and he now loathes the Eve in Marya. He is for the moment a hurt boy-child. Now an Eve becomes Mother Mary: "She put her warm hand over his firmly and said: 'My little Stephan, don't worry' " (*Q*, 186), and they are off to another hotel and the train out of Paris. How well Rhys understood and could express the binary and contradictory function of women in the lives of men.

Marya as the Other

A contemporary reader may ask, why didn't Marya simply find a job to support herself? There are several reasons. She is an Englishwoman married to a Polish man who has lived in Paris four years without employment in a time when respectable middle-class wives or those aspiring to middle-class status were to be supported by their husbands and not expected to be gainfully employed. "Suddenly and ruthlessly" she is "transplanted," like a heroine in a Zola novel, from "solid comfort to the hazards of Montmartre" (*Q*, 15). Even when Stephan is in prison, having left her with practically no funds, he never suggests that she find some work. Instead he urges her to move in with and stay with the seemingly respectable, kind-hearted couple who are offering her protection. From his male viewpoint she is less likely to get into trouble, to be seduced into prostitution, to damage his marital property, to injure his pride and manhood, if she is safely deposited in a bourgeois household and protected by another marriage. Early in the novel, when Stephan is courting Marya the chorus girl and learns that she is penniless, he states wisely and prophetically, "It's better when a woman has some money, I think. It's much safer for her" (*Q*, 19).

The possibilities of meaningful, respectable employment are few for Marya. Her work experience prior to her marriage was "several years as a member of Mr. Albert Prance's No.1 touring company" in England (*Q*, 15). She was not star material and she sang in a quavering voice. Stage work in Paris was not likely even if Stephan would have approved. Lois keeps holding out the possibility of a reference to a couturier where Marya could work as a mannequin, but that is merely bait in the trap.

Marya tries to obtain financial aid from an aunt in England, but only a few pounds are forthcoming, along with the gratuitous advice that she visit "the British clergyman resident in Paris" (*Q*, 58). Besides being a foreign woman, Marya is an Other in a way peculiar to Rhys's fiction. Although Marya is the sole Rhys heroine in the novels who is identified clearly as English or European, the narrator nevertheless seems to imply that Marya is not totally English. Perhaps Rhys herself is unconsciously connecting with her own colonial and mixed national and possibly racial inheritance. Marya is oblivious to being an ethnic, colonial, or racial Other, but other Others seem to sense it. Rhys describes Marya as "a blond girl, not very tall, slender-waisted. Her face was short, high cheek-boned, full-lipped; her long eyes slanted upwards towards the temples and were gentle and oddly remote in expression. Often on the Boulevards St. Michel and Montparnasse shabby youths would glide up to her and address her hopefully in unknown and spitting tongues. When they were very shabby she would smile in a distant manner and answer in English: 'I'm very sorry; I don't understand what you're saying' " (Q, 5). The description is of Rhys at that time of her life. That some non-French, non-English, seemingly non-European people recognize Marya as a possible compatriot implies a hidden (from Marya, too) racial Otherness. Later in the text, when she is nearly hysterical in the hotel room in which she entertains Heidler, she collapses on the bed: "He knelt down and stared at her. Her head had dropped backwards over the edge of the bed and from that angle her face seemed strange to him: the cheek bones looked higher and more prominent, the nostrils wider, the lips thicker. A strange little Kalmuck face" (Q, 131). Heidler sees her upside down face as a Mongolian face. The implication of the contact with the foreigners on the street and Heidler's comment is that Rhys wants us to see Marya as exotic looking, to a degree a non-European and by implication racially different.

Marya is of course an Other in a very obvious way: she is an "other woman," the third party to a marriage, and the marriage partners "assume their prerogative to inflict pain upon her" (Emery, 109). Quickly enough in this tale of a six month affair, Heidler, his lust for sex and power temporarily satisfied by the used up Marya, sees her as a "diseased Other" (Emery, 111). The "lover" says to Marya, "I have a horror of you. When I think of you I feel sick" (Q, 148).

In a sense Marya is permanently ill, permanently wounded, even from birth. In the context of Heidler's phallocentric society, she can never be whole in body or in spirit. He alone in his relationships has the complete ego. Some women may be healthy. The narrator says of a woman at the Bal du Printemps, "She was very healthy looking . . . with long, very sharp teeth" (Q, 70). Only with the ability to bite and hurt can a woman remain healthy. Only as a well-equipped animal can a woman survive in the Parisian jungle.

A Failure of Sisterhood

Where is female friendship? Where are Marya's true friends? Why does she not seem to have real woman friends? Why is it that Cairn, a male without money and therefore impotent, is the only person to take a little pity on a confused, lost, trapped person? The first woman "friend" of Marya's we meet in the text is Esther De Solla, a mediocre painter. She leads Marya to the Heidlers. Later, when her husband is arrested, Marya immediately thinks of Esther: " 'I must go and find De Solla. . . .' Her mind clung desperately to the thought of Miss De Solla's calm, her deep and masculine voice" (Q, 25). It is the thought of Esther's "masculine" qualities that temporarily gives Marya hope, not her sisterhood, but De Solla has left for London.

Later Marya meets Esther again and informs her that she is living with the people she introduced her to. "As a matter of fact I heard you were," Esther says coldly (Q, 68). And then she cuts her. Marya is now outside the pale of respectability. De Solla disapproves and won't compromise her own position by continuing her comradeship with a friend in trouble.

Lois, of course, is a sexual quisling. Despite the initial appearance of comity, she, the wife, and Marya, the lover, must be enemies. They are at war.

When Marya is sent by Heidler to Cannes for rest and to get her out of his hair for a while, she is "befriended" by Miss Nicolson, a landscape painter in the Heidler crowd whom Marya has previously met and whom Rhys describes in wonderful detail, down to her small feet, which "were shod with crocodile-skin shoes. It was oddly shocking to catch glimpses of very hairy legs through her thin silk stockings" (Q, 158). The image of the hairy, male-appearing legs symbolizes Miss Nicolson's role as a betrayer of the young woman to patriarchal power. Ostensibly concerned for Marya's health and well-being, she is really a spy for Lois, and she causes Marya to spend her last few francs on a meal for her.

To put it bluntly, there is no sisterhood in Rhys's picture of early twentieth-century life. Among the bourgeoisie, women are only competitors: those comfortably protected within the dominant patriarchal system plot to keep the others out or allow them in only on surrender terms; those without struggle to get in.

Among the Bohemians the amorality of their culture also betrayed women. Sexual freedom without commitment is only to the male's advantage. With God dead and religion a sham, no moral code gave even a minimum protection to women like Marya. And the Heidlers, both bourgeois and Bohemian, were doubly dangerous.

Characterization

Quartet can be considered as an existentialist novel, a study of loneliness even in crowds, of isolation, of noncommunication, of a world in which existence has no meaning beyond itself. It depicts the existential precept that one is responsible for one's actions even if one cannot foresee their consequences. Carole Angier also notes that although the novel's view of life is harsh, it is "also sentimental, and above all it absolves Marya of any responsibility. People are cruel, and she has no money or power; so she is exploited. *That* is why the terrible things happen. Beyond that it is simply fate, and no one knows where we are going" (Angier, 188). There is much to agree with in Angier's statement, but perhaps it is too simplistic and apologetic.

The triumvir against Marya, the unwitting allies—Heidler, Lois, Stephan—are overwhelmingly powerful. They, more than fate, control her, and the novel does not seem to absolve Marya of any responsibility but rather punishes her unfairly but realistically for her hard-to-avoid transgressions. Still, Marya has courage, as do all of Rhys's heroines. She fights back—ineffectually, yes; pitifully yes—but she fights. Even without the aid of masculine argumentation and spoken language, she rises to one powerful moment of woman's rage just before her husband throws her to the floor. "She began to laugh at him insultingly. Suddenly he had become the symbol of everything that all her life had baffled and tortured her. Her only idea was to find words that would hurt him—vile words to scream at him" (*Q*, 184). She becomes a virago in what may be the last act of her life, for in her transformational epiphany she understands that it is male control of the structure of thought and the social order that has "baffled and tortured" her (Staley, 53).

But although Marya is trapped in the language of the dominant discourse, the novel, indeed all the Rhys novels, are not. The interior discourses in Rhys present an unprecedented world "of women's speech, of women talking back, saying what they *want* to say, in the interstices of the 'real' dialogue."[3] This is a major political and technical achievement of Rhys's *Quartet* and a process that stayed with her.

When near the end of the novel Marya allows a young man to pick
her up and take her to his room and bed, she does so not only because
she is depressed—"Why not? . . . What does it matter" (*Q*, 152)—but
also because she chooses to have sex this time, and not with Heidler nor
Zelli. The act is a secret unconscious or conscious betrayal and revenge
against the men who hold tyrannical power over her. Of course Hugh,
Lois, and Stephan are just as trapped as Marya is within the dominant
discourse and values that regulate their existence. Their acts are legis-
lated within the sexual and cultural politics of the 1920s. They too must
play their requisite positions in the social game. They too must sing
their respective parts in the quartet until the sad song ends.

Marya is so unprepared; she has not been educated or trained for the
battle of the sexes or the war with the world. Marya is a tragic heroine:
not perfect, weak-willed, an adulterer, flawed, but doomed not only by
her flaws but also by an inexorable fate that is both hers as an individual
and that of women generally in her time.

The three other main characters of the novel are lined up in opposi-
tion. The hateful, lascivious Heidler hasn't a single redeeming character-
istic. He is a prototypical male monster, the user and abuser of the
female as slave. He has spent his life with artists and yet seems devoid of
creativity, but then he does not produce art, he sells it. The progress of
his life is to go from one self-indulgence to another. He is full of self-
importance and self-pity, an Oriental potentate in a society that creates
them wholesale out of money, immorality, and selfishness. The insensi-
tivity and immobility of the man are clear in the narrator's first description of Heidler: "He looked as if nothing could break him down. He was
a tall, fair man of perhaps forty-five. His shoulders were tremendous, his
nose arrogant, his hands short, broad and so plump that the knuckles
were dimpled. The wooden expression of his face was carefully striven
for. His eyes were light blue and intelligent, but with a curious underly-
ing expression of obtuseness—even of brutality" (*Q*, 11). Pathetically,
Marya, the fly approaching the spider, thinks, "I expect he's awfully
fussy" (*Q*, 11). Little does she know then how "fussy" he could be.

Though she is a fool to put up with Heidler, Lois commands some
sympathy despite her role as high priestess of betrayal. She does love
Heidler, difficult as it is for the reader to understand her feeling. She is
completely dependent on her husband's financial support. She has no
children. She has no integrity when it comes to Heidler's philandering.
She has a masochistic streak that her marital relationship seems to sati-
ate. During the 1920s psychoanalysts and intellectuals debated the

cause of what they saw as a degree of masochism in modern Western women. Was it pathological, or socially conditioned, or a part of women's physiological nature? (Emery, 116). Lois and Marya allow Heidler to abuse them. For Freud, female masochism was both "natural" and neurotic, but surely, if Rhys joined in the debate, her position was that female masochism was conditioned and not a pathology or indeed a genetically programmed means of obtaining female submission to male penetration.

Lois seems also to have a sadistic side, as when she aids Heidler in tormenting Marya. She says to him, "Let's go to Luna-Park after dinner. . . . We'll put Mado on the joy wheel, and watch her being banged about a bit. Well, she ought to amuse us sometimes; she ought to sing for her supper; that's what she's here for, isn't it?" (Q, 85). The image is that what is a joy wheel for Lois is a torture wheel for Marya, with Lois and Hugh voyeuristically enjoying the spectacle. The fact that this "other woman" is the object of their desires, sexual for Heidler and sadomasochistic for Lois, gives them, in their own minds, the right to torment her. Lois paints Marya's portrait to add to the gallery of Heidler victims.

Lois is plump, dark, and younger than Heidler but not a beauty. Her eyes are beautiful, "clearly brown, the long lashes curving upwards, but there was a suspicious, almost a deadened look to them" (Q, 11). She has reason to be suspicious of both her husband and of other women, and the parade of humiliating experiences at the hands of Heidler surely deadened her look. In talking to Marya about Heidler, Lois's subtext is, "D'you suppose that I care what you are, or think or feel? I'm talking about the man, the male, the important person, the only person who matters" (Q, 81). Lois is sure that women are inferior to men. Rhys would have it that this is the "wives" position, the Victorian "good woman's" view, the result of a century of indoctrination.[4] The name *Lois* means "battle-maiden" (Nebeker, 11), and she will fight Marya and any other woman who seems an antagonist. She is "formidable, very formidable, an instrument made, exactly shaped and sharpened for one purpose" (Q, 97), and that purpose is to do battle in mortal combat with other women and give no quarter. She would be amazed and scornful to learn that Marya said to Heidler, "Be kind to Lois" (Q, 106).

Stephan, although young, vital, and handsome, is "secretive, and a liar, but he was a very gentle and expert lover" (Q, 22). He is also a thief, and a weak and amoral person who gambles not only with his own life but with his wife's. His selfishness has few bounds. In the hotel room in which they make their "home" when he is released from prison, he complains when nervously she tears a cigarette: "Don't strew tobacco on my bed, Marya" (Q, 137). The bed is his, not theirs. In the end, when Stephan finally physically attacks his wife, the once "loving" husband becomes another male monster. Stephan's vile character is fully exposed when the outrage he felt over being betrayed by Marya and Heidler is shown to be hypocritical as he departs to start a new life with another woman (Q, 186).

In *Quartet* Rhys has created four finely drawn major characters who live through and seemingly beyond the pages. All but Marya seem beyond redemption, and she may be dead. They are exemplars of an oppressive ideology; raw, unmitigated capitalism with its concomitant bourgeois avarice, selfishness, and immorality. They vouchsafe nothing. They seldom or never have a thought about social responsibilities, ethics, right and wrong, or the suffering of others. Their saving grace is that they are, after all, vividly realistic portraits of human beings like us.

The Theme of Confinement

The quartet are all in prison. All are in cages. Early twentieth-century artistic society thought it was politically, materialistically, and sexually free because it could not see the parameters of the cage: residual Victorian attitudes toward sexual relations, sexuality, and marriage, and hypocritical bourgeois values.

The most obvious prisoner is Stephan. He is a criminal and he goes to the Santé and then to the prison at Fresnes, where of course he is treated harshly and where he also suffers because his wife has no way of supporting herself. Even more painful for him, she, as his property, is subject to appropriation by one or several other males, thus injuring his male hubris. He understands that to be trapped once is to be a prisoner forever. When Marya, visiting him in prison, says, "If anybody tried to catch me and lock me up I'd fight like a wild animal; I'd fight till they let me out or till I died" (Q, 136). He replies, "Oh, no, you wouldn't, not for long, believe me. You'd do as the others do—you'd wait and be a wild animal when you came out. . . . but you don't come out. Nobody ever comes out" (Q, 136).

The Heidlers are prisoners in and of their marriage, forced to play hypocritical roles for the benefit of society's requirement of "appearance." Marya is tricked into a term of confinement at hard labor and psychological torture within that prison/marriage of which Lois and

H. J. are the trustees and whose pleasure is the power they have over the erotically charged, ambiguous figure of a marginalized woman. Marya is a prisoner whose "crimes" may be passivity, amorality, and simply being a woman. She is not only a prisoner in the Heidler marriage, she is incarcerated in her own. She feels sympathy, responsibility, and residual love for her imprisoned husband. She believes that she is supposed to have these feelings and is appalled when Lois and H. J. try to separate her from them. Of course, Stephan is unworthy of her sympathy and sacrifice.

The iterative symbol of Marya's incarceration is the "room," the Other's room, the cage for the girl slave in the Heidler household, the hotel rooms she shares with her husband, and the hotel room Heidler sets her up in as his mistress, where she and other, later Rhys heroines live, wait, sleep, eat, drink, smoke, and fornicate when men come. It is in the Heidler-paid room at the Hôtel du Bosphore that Marya comes to understand the truth of her predicament and how common her woman's experience is, when she imagines "All the women who had lain where she was lying" (Q, 119).

The room at the Heidlers' would at first seem comfortable as a zoo cage may feel at first to a wild animal captured in trauma and trucked to imprisonment in fear and terror. There would be food, some peace after being hunted, and time to rest. Slowly the sense of loss of freedom, boredom, the constriction of space, and the feeling of degradation set in, followed by desperation and then extreme and continued tiredness.

Rhys presents Marya's prisoner status symbolically when she and Miss Nicolson visit the zoo in Nice, where they see "a young fox in a cage . . . perhaps three yards long. Up and down it ran, up and down, and Marya imagined that each time it turned it did so with a certain hopefulness, as if it thought that escape was possible. Then, of course, there were the bars. It would strike its nose, turn and run again. Up and down, up and down, ceaselessly. A horrible sight, really" (Q, 160). Marya understands that she is a young, trapped animal. Her companion says, "Sweet thing." The words apply to either the girl or the fox.

Paris is the larger physical prison. As a huge metropolis, of course, it is impersonal and unfriendly. But Marya seems to expect more of it. She (and Rhys) saw it first as "The City of Light," a place millions who would never see Paris dreamed about and wished to live in. They were fascinated by the young artists' world of Montparnasse and Montmartre: "The lights winking up at a pallid moon, the slender painted ladies, the wings of the Moulin Rouge, the smell of petrol and perfume and cooking. The Place Blanche, Paris, Life itself" (*Q,* 23). Could a place be more lovable and loved?

But as soon as her husband is taken away to prison and she is deprived of masculine protection and support, the city turns dangerous, a jungle of a few strong and the many weak, an unhealthy, amoral place where Marya is quickly compromised and taken ill. Marya fears the life of the streets. The city is labyrinthine, and gargoyles roam it. The expatriate Bohemian world to which she gravitates as an Englishwoman, the milieu of Hemingway's *The Sun Also Rises* (1926), is predatory and amoral. It is a place of ennui, a tired, war-exhausted place where only sex and breaking rules are exciting.

Marya knows that without money or an adequately paying job she will wind up performing in degrading shows or working as a prostitute. Her own unconsidered amorality is a significant handicap, and in a way, she does become a prostitute to the Heidlers, ultimately as Heidler's troublesome sexual slave, spending her days waiting for him in a hotel room. In the end the identity of Paris is reduced to a place of bedrooms and hotel rooms, and finally the hotel room that Stephan locates for Marya and himself "near the Gare du Nord" (*Q,* 166), where Stephan at last attacks Marya and leaves her for dead as he takes up with the prostitute Mademoiselle Chardin. In the heartlessly cruel ending of *Quartet,* the reader comes to realize that the Paris of the novel is more Zola's than Collette's.

But Rhys's Paris of the 1920s, as portrayed in *Quartet,* is also a grand Bakhtian carnival of cruelty where the masks of the people no longer prefigure regeneration of communal structure and support, as they did in the Middle Ages, but now exist for intrigue, deception, and treachery, so that a helpless girl may be turned into a tragic doll.[5] Still the bacchanalia aspects of the bar and café life of Montmartre resemble the true carnival: the music, the drinking, the feasting—"men in caps and hatless girls cling together, shake themselves and turn with abandon" (*Q,* 69) at the Bal du Printemps. Carnival and Bacchanal are prelude to the archetypal rite of spring, sex, thus providing these jaded moderns, to the narrator's amazement, "a certain amount of genuine enjoyment" (*Q,* 69).

Narrative Technique

Although *Quartet* is written in the third person, the text creates the distinct impression that the narrator and the heroine are one. The narrator is, of course, not necessarily the author; one can have a multi-level narration: the author, the constructed author presenting herself or himself in a desired way, a constructed narrator different from the author, and a heroine or hero through whose eyes we experience the text (the reader-listener may also be divided into several constructs). In this novel, author, narrator, and heroine do seem to blend into one. The modernist value of retaining objective distance from the persona and plot is weakened. A Romantic subjectivism is in conflict with modernist objectivity, but the novel does not suffer for this vacillation. According to their critical perspectives and persuasions, critics divide on the efficacy and appropriateness of this aspect of Rhys's narrative technique in the earlier novels. Nevertheless, *Quartet* is definitely well positioned in the canon of modernist novels, with its conscious artistry, psychological manifestations, allusive content, symbolic levels, and diminished emphasis on plot and dramatic action central to the traditional, late nineteenth and early twentieth-century novel.

Quartet is cinematic, as if it had been conceived in film shots and sequences. Chapters are short, some a page long. Longer chapters are subdivided by a row of asterisks. The number of locales are few, as if a screen play were being produced, or even a stage play. The writing is sparse, sharp, and understated, like a scenario or treatment, and divided into passages of dialogue followed by action descriptions and settings, like a film script. The events in the play occur in a matter of months, and time passes between scenes. This passage is made quickly clear as the next scene opens. In cinematic terms Rhys edits by using the quick cut.

The novel's point of view is simple and consistent: Marya's perspective on her life. Time is past but the action feels immediate. Tension is not only sustained but builds from episode to episode as Marya's inevitable fate closes in on her, and we see her fall before the cleverness, the intrigue, and the inexorable power of Heidler.

Marya's interior monologues, like Shakespearean soliloquies, form a major architectonic of the text, as when she is waiting in the hotel room for Heidler and is disgusted with what she has allowed herself to become: " 'What's the matter with you? . . . Why are you like this? Why can't you be clever? Pull yourself together. . . . No self-control,' thought Marya. 'That's what's the matter with me, No training' " (*Q*, 117).

The rhythm of the novel changes from the early, cool, logical consciousness of the narrator and the realistic description to the distressed, distraught, feverish, dreamlike reflections of the desperate Marya. An early flashback economically establishes Marya's background, her first

employment as a chorus girl, how she came to meet Stephan Zelli in
London, their courtship, and their coming to Paris. Perhaps these cinematic possibilities caused the Merchant Ivory Film Company to choose
Quartet as the first Rhys novel to be made into a motion picture (1981)
and helped the director, John Ivory, and the screenwriter, the distinguished novelist Ruth Prawer Jhabvala, to prepare a fine and faithful
script.

Imagery

With its iterative value, structural function, and thematic weight, the
imagery in *Quartet* approaches poetry's usage. The key iterative, architectonic, and symbolic image in *Quartet* is the animal image. Paula Le
Gallez points out that early in the text Rhys establishes Marya as "a displaced sheep, doomed to follow the leader, but never quite making it
into the group,"[6] citing the reported ironic conversation with the Heidlers by Miss De Solla: "They discussed eating, cooking, England and,
finally, Marya, whom they spoke of in the third person as if she were a
strange animal or at any rate a strayed animal—one not quite of the
fold" (*Q*, 11). The conversation takes place in Marya's immediate presence, as if she were without understanding, let alone feeling, in other
words as if she were a sheep for shearing, or perhaps a vulnerable foreigner, an Other not understanding the language. Her meekness seals
her fate.

Previously we have seen how the fox in the zoo cage symbolizes
Marya's predicament (*Q*, 160). The pacing, frustrated animal parallels
and pictures Marya's psychological distress and vacillations. More significantly, the extended image serves as the keystone for the structural
device of the iterative animal image: to be precise, the image of the
trapped animal. This is what Marya is. In the most basic way and yet on
the most abstract allegorical level, the trapping and incarceration of a
human animal is what *Quartet* is about.

As a trapped animal Marya seeks any way out of her cage, not being
able to see ahead that some seeming exits are not escapes but part of the
labyrinthine trap she is in, as when she is under siege by Heidler and she
is so hungry for some relief, some joy, that she is open to try anything:
" 'How have I stood it so long?' And her longing for joy, for any joy, for
any pleasure was a mad thing in her heart. It was sharp like pain and she
clenched her teeth. It was like some splendid caged animal roused and
fighting to get out" (*Q*, 74). When Heidler gets into Marya's bedroom,

"she was in a frenzy of senseless fright. Fright of a child shut up in a dark room. Fright of an animal caught in a trap" (Q, 90). The very heart of Marya is the incarcerated animal desperate for freedom. When she is caged in the hotel room Heidler pays for, her keeper has broken her spirit. Marya "was quivering and abject in his arms, like some unfortunate dog abasing itself before its master" (Q, 131). A metaphysical dimension exists in Quartet within the implied question: are all women, indeed all human beings, mere trapped animals controlled by other forces—biological determinism, genetic predestination, economic determinism, nature, fate, God? At least in the kingdom of patriarchy every woman, even the exalted wifelike Lois, is a "well-trained domestic animal" (Q,107). Interestingly, Rhys's ascribing, with conscious irony, the animal image to her heroine replicates Heidler's dehumanization of Marya in his use of her as a sexual creature over which, he believes, he has rightful, God-given dominion.

Another significant iterative image in Quartet and elsewhere in Rhys's work is the water image. Water usually symbolizes life, but in Rhys, from Quartet to Wide Sargasso Sea, the tenor is always death, violent death by drowning. When Stephan is arrested, Marya goes to Esther for help, only to find that the artist has left for London. It is raining, the pavements are "slippery and glistening, with pools of water here and there" (Q, 26). Returning, she sees the Heidlers sheltering themselves beneath a huge umbrella, but she has no shelter now and people "stared at her because she was walking so slowly in the pouring rain" (Q, 26). The streets of Paris, a city divided by a river, are dangerous, even deadly places for a woman alone, and Paris is a place one could drown in. Later, when she feels "quite dead," the streets seem to her to be water, in which she had drowned: "As she walked back to the hotel after her meal, Marya would have the strange sensation that she was walking under water . . . the sound of water was in her ears" (Q, 123).

When Stephan returns from prison and Marya finds herself still imagining herself being watched by Heidler as she undresses, "her obsession gripped her, arid, torturing, gigantic, possessing her as utterly as the longing for water possesses someone who is dying of thirst" (Q, 145). The water that Marya wants is the water of oblivion. There are two kinds of death for Rhys's women, the biological death and the emotional one that is the result of being tangled up in relationships and being dragged down. Her women all endure the latter before they suffer the former. The sea can be "caressing," Marya thinks: "If you were anything else but a tired-out coward, you'd swim out into the blue and

never come back. A good way to finish if you'd made a mess of your life"
(*Q*, 164).

Conclusion

In *Quartet* Jean Rhys found an original voice and took control of the
images, themes, and techniques she would employ in all of her subsequent novels. She mastered the psychological woman's novel in her first
try. Speaking of Rhys and *Quartet,* Thomas F. Staley says that "The economy of language and directness of style can lead us to underestimate the
range, depth, and quality of feeling in her work, but her narrative focus
and technique relieve the intense subjectivity in *Quartet* and offer a dramatic, human portrait of the female consciousness in the modern
world."[7]

Quartet is Jean Rhys's "homiletic on the plight of women in a world
corrupted by men" (Nebeker, 13). The novel implies that investing in
men is unwise, but some women cannot but help doing it. The more
traditionally and passively feminine a woman is, and the stronger she
thinks she is when she is young and attractive, the more tempting and
vulnerable a target of acquisition she is. Rhys seems to be saying to
other women, "This is what happens to us even when we are young and
desirable; especially when we are young and desirable. We are born victims." *Quartet* shows the sexual revolution of the twentieth century as
far from complete. Misogyny is alive and well. Marriage still rules the
sexual life of women but not of men. Sex is not so pleasurable. It is
bartered for "love" and security. Again and again Marya says of it,
"What does it matter?" Women are classified binarily: good or bad,
married or single, whores or husband stealers. Subconsciously, Rhys
sees married European women as little different from the wives of plantation owners in the West Indies, who were expected to be faithful to
their husbands while their husbands had uninhibited access to the
Other women of their world: slaves before emancipation, and, in Rhys's
time, black female youths, servants, and agricultural workers (Emery,
120). Lastly, Rhys implies that a woman's life with a man is always
dangerous. Even when the relationship is exciting and is going well,
Marya dreads "not desertion, but some vague, dimly apprehended catastrophe" (*Q*, 22).

Marya and other young women in the Rhys canon are commodities.
Alicia Borinsky states that attractive young women are illusionists with
makeup and clothes. Their femininity is more about money than sex.[8]

They desire to be mannequins, but they are mannequins, artifacts created to be painted, and on which to hang erotically stimulating clothes to entice sales of garments or bodies. The flapper slip dresses Marya wears even when she is shivering with cold are to show off the wares. The barrier between her and others is "precarious" (Borinsky, 297).

Quartet is a remarkable first novel, a fiery, passionate story that nevertheless is told with control, lucidity, and appropriate distance. It is part satire, part exposé, and part realistic description of an artistic community in a fascinating and famous time and place. Although there is evil in the story, it is not a morality play. The weak and the strong are both predatory, although the strong are better at it and have the advantages of money and power. Charming and attractive young people help create their own doom.

Quartet adds up to a small but unforgettable jewel of an early modernist novel. Contemporary feminists now read *Quartet* as a frightening warning to women to inventory and nurture one's resources and not to fall into a possession.

Chapter Four
After Leaving Mr. Mackenzie

After Leaving Mr. Mackenzie is a dark and forbidding novel of a woman descending into existential despair as the aimlessness and the purposelessness of her life leads her, via the betrayal of lovers and abandonment by family, to alcoholism, promiscuity, and a hellish depth of degradation. The trajectory of the woman's fall is through drunkenness, loss of self-respect, wild behavior, recklessness, irresponsibility, and finally total capitulation to male sexual power. It is a novel without love, only the debris of love.

After Leaving Mr. Mackenzie is also the story of a woman in deepening exile from her home, culture, sisterhood, womanhood, humanity, and her very self. It paints an unmitigated picture of early twentieth-century European life as vicious, heartless, exploiting, selfish, and cruel. It despairs for woman's survival. It depicts the feminine consciousness as a living nightmare. Most simply put, its frightening thesis is that a woman's greatest fear is the loss of sexual attractiveness through growing older. In other words her false friend, really her greatest enemy, is her own vulnerable body. In *After Leaving Mr. Mackenzie* the values, lives, hopes, and expectations of women and men are more separate and distinct than in any other Rhys novel except *Wide Sargasso Sea*. Reviews generally recognized Rhys's growth and achievement as a novelist in *After Leaving Mr. Mackenzie*, especially when they compared it to *Quartet* (Angier, 240). Words like *superb* and *flawless* were used by major British and American reviewers, and they commented that it had "the balance and the beauty of verse" (Angier, 280). A few, less attuned to modernist subjects, considered the novel "a waste of talent" in a "sordid little story" (Angier, 280).

After Leaving Mr. Mackenzie is a carefully structured tale of two cities: Paris and London. It is divided into three parts, a long Paris segment, a longer London segment, and a short concluding episode back in Paris. Julia Martin is a pathetically masochistic woman in her mid thirties, a Marya Zelli at the next stage of her life, just possibly English, living hand-to-mouth in Paris. She is a frail reed broken by the world and the betrayal of her most recent lover, Mackenzie, who has thrown her over six months ago, leaving her to live off weekly checks his lawyers send her. Julia had once been married and had a son who died. She left her husband because "it seemed natural."[1] Although she had sometimes worked as an artist's model and a mannequin, Julia has almost always lived off the money men have given her: from Mr. James when she was 19 and living in London, from Mackenzie recently in Paris, and from the new admirer, Mr. Horsfield, who gives her money in Paris and sends her money later from London when she finally returns to Paris as the novel concludes. Even when her mother is dying and she meets her old uncle again in London, she asks him for money. In between James and Mackenzie there were "five or six" others.

It is in Paris in springtime when the novel opens. Julia is an angry, bitter, jilted lover, a discarded kept woman who has just received an extra large but final payment from Mackenzie. She waits for Mackenzie outside his flat and then tails him to a restaurant where she is determined to "have it out with him" (*ALMM*, 22). She sits down at his table, where to cover his embarrassment he offers her a drink. After an uncomfortable conversation she impetuously returns the final check and then "picked up her glove and hit his cheek with it, but so lightly that he did not even blink. 'I despise you,' she said" (*ALMM*, 34). Her gesture of disdain and her attempt to regain some self-respect is gallant in its nature. The glove across the cheek both challenges and defeats what little manhood there is in this weak and selfish man. However, Julia is now without cash or income.

But Julia's activities have been observed by another patron in the restaurant, a vacationing English businessman, George Horsfield, who is taken with Julia and quickly finds her in another café shortly after the incident with Mackenzie. Physically attracted to Julia and feeling compassion, he gives her the same amount of money she has just thrown away. With it she buys clothes and goes to London to look up her first and most sympathetic lover, James, who has never failed to help her, but who, the reader realizes, is the man who seduced her at the age of 19 and led her into the life of the demimonde. Julia also makes contact with her family, and by chance she arrives as her mother lays dying. She tries unsuccessfully to communicate with her mother and to reconcile with her sister Norah. Despite the seeming emphasis on love affairs, the episodes with mother and sister are the central events in the narrative.

Julia also expects to see Horsfield in London, and she is not disappointed. They become lovers, but her despair over her mother's death, the rejection by James in a way similar to how she was paid off by Mackenzie, and her growing alcohol-induced lethargy, along with Horsfield's diffidence and indecisiveness, conspire to destroy the relationship. Julia returns to Paris and begins to fall apart. A small, final sum and a farewell arrive from Horsfield in London. She contemplates suicide by jumping into the Seine but rejects that solution. The novel ends with Julia first being turned down by a younger man and then finding Mackenzie in a café, drinking with him, and once more "borrowing" some money from him.

A Woman's Isolation

What does Julia Martin want? It is never stated. She may not know herself, which of course implies that Rhys does not know what her character wants. It may be that she wants marriage or some type of permanently committed relationship in which she will be loved and adored for the rest of her life by a sympathetic, affluent man who will indulge her whims, tolerate her drinking, and keep her in the fashionable clothes she so adores. It may be that she merely wants to be happy, to experience joy, and not to be lonely again. Perhaps she wants a different world, in which men do not have all the power and where language is not controlled by them, and women's "speak" is as acceptable as male "speak," so that she could at last tell her story and validate her existence without having to translate it into the male linguistic and narrative system.

Perhaps she unconsciously desires to be "demythologized" as an archetypal "woman" so that she can for once control her own image and her own body, and find and be what really is beneath the makeup, the clothes, the hairdos, the lying to and pleasing of men, the seemingly required seeking of and rejecting seduction, and the deadly competition with other women for the scraps from the patriarchal table. Finally, perhaps she suffers in her loneliness and isolation from, in Freudian terms, the child's desire to merge with her mother, to return home, "to enter the mother's terrain."[2]

Julia is an exile. She has been an exile from England, having taken up residence in Europe upon marriage. She is an exile and estranged from her family from possibly as far back as when she was 19, when she had become a chorus girl and was the kept mistress of James. Since her mother's nationality is unsure, Julia's seems to be, also. She may be the child of colonials, perhaps born outside of England. She thinks "of the dark shadows of houses in a street white with sunshine," and she is

described as having "the hands of an oriental" (*ALMM*, 12, 13). Rhys
chooses to let that be obscure. "Her career of ups and downs had rubbed
most of the hall-marks off her, so that it was not easy to guess at her
age, her nationality, or the social background to which she properly
belonged" (*ALMM*, 14).

Julia is in exile from the respectable bourgeois world because of the
lifestyle choices she has made or that have been thrust upon her. Without female friends she is in exile from the world of women; she is a chat-
tel in the masculine world. That world has taught her to distrust, even
hate other women. While in an elevator Julia sees a girl standing next to
her, staring persistently. "She grew angry and thought: 'Well, I can stare
too. . . .' She narrowed her eyes and glared. The girl was short and
slim. . . . Some fool probably thought her pretty" (*ALMM*, 119). The
girl turns her back on Julia. " 'Bad luck to you then,' thought Julia.
'Bad luck to you' " (*ALMM*, 120). She is quick to be angry with women
on the vaguest appearance of a slight, but facing men and being angry
with them is infinitely more difficult for her. She has the wrong enemies,
only because they are easier to hate—young women because they are
young and therefore a threat—and to despise—old women because they
are old and therefore contemptible.

Julia seems even to be an exile from herself, from that part of her that
has confidence in her ability to get by on her own efforts and skills as
dancer and model, to attract men with her looks and sex appeal, and to
be a part of a mutually supportive family.

Clearly the central theme of *After Leaving Mr. Mackenzie* is the isolation of a woman. Julia is so alone. Despite the fact that much of her
adult life has been spent living with men or being kept by them, it is
apparent that she is lonely within the relationships, too. Her deep,
pathological loneliness stems from the totality of her failed relationships.
In a sense the novel is a catalog of failed and failing relationships, and
the most significant failures are not in the heterosexual narrative that
appears to be foregrounded by the novelist or in the familial train wreck
that is symbolized by Julia's disastrous encounter with her parsimonious
Uncle Griffiths, but in the monumental failure of the mother-daughter
dyad and the auxiliary sister-sister dyad.

Mother and Daughter

Julia's mother spent her childhood in Brazil, but there is no evidence
that Mrs. Griffiths was Brazilian or that she lived there after her youth.

Somehow, and at some unknown time, she came to England, where often she "was sickening for the sun" (*ALMM,* 105). Julia remembers her mother saying of England, "This is a cold, grey country. This isn't a country to be really happy in" (*ALMM,* 105), which was precisely Rhys's feeling about life in England. All of Rhysland, except for the Antilles, is a cold place growing colder. As a child Julia "had woven innumerable romances about her mother's childhood in South America" (*ALMM,* 105), but her mother had answered her "innumerable questions . . . inadequately or not at all, for she was an inarticulate woman" (*ALMM,* 105). Mother and daughter have difficulty not only in communicating with each other but in articulating their stories in the language of the dominant discourse.

But where is Julia's geography? Ostensibly she is "English," but her family connections in England appear to be very few. Is she colonial born? Was her mother an Englishwoman born in South America who spent her childhood there as the daughter of businesspeople or diplomats? Rhys is purposefully vague in her sparse offering of information, always teasing the reader, who wants a little more, and must use her or his imagination to end enigmas.

What Julia most wants from her dying mother, and what it is impossible for her now to receive, is past love from a warm, embracing woman preferring her to others and approving of her. She cannot ask her comatose mother anything. She cannot explain her sad life and what has happened to her. She can only "whisper soundlessly: 'Oh, darling, there's something I want to explain to you. You must listen' " (*ALMM,* 98), but her mother cannot hear, and anyway she is whispering soundlessly. It is the mother who begins to "cry, loudly and disconsolately, like a child" (*ALMM,* 98–99). The mumbling and moaning and groans of her mother place Julia in the maternal position. It is not a totally strange one to her, as she had given birth once to a son who died as an infant because of the poverty she and her husband endured.

Although mother and daughter have changed roles, they remain incommunicative. Significantly, Julia is a child in need of her mother's love, Mrs. Griffiths has reverted to a childhood role of utter dependency, and sister Norah is an angry, put-upon child. Is Rhys implying that early twentieth-century European society decreed that all women must remain in the childhood state of emotional and economic dependency?

When Julia witnesses the cremation of her mother's body at Golders Green, she is temporarily freed from the longing for merging with or reentering her mother's body: "In a miraculous manner some essence of her was shooting upwards like a flame. She was great. She was a defiant flame shooting upwards not to plead but to threaten" (*ALMM*, 131). Her mother's death momentarily liberates her. She is a woman, not a child. She has power and strength for an instant, but as one never truly and fully separates from childhood and parents, Julia comes down from her freedom high quickly: "Then the flame sank down again, useless, having reached nothing" (*ALMM*, 131). Society has not changed; Julia's life has not changed.

Sisters

Norah is Julia's younger sister. The natural competition between two same-sex siblings has been exacerbated by the different lives the sisters have lived. Julia has existed on the fringes of society as a model and as a demimondaine. Her return visit is as an unwelcome prodigal, whereas Norah, an unhappy woman whose recent "life has been slavery" (*ALMM*, 104), conceives herself as the "good daughter" and has remained close to her mother. She wants life out in the warm, vibrant, larger world, but as Deborah Kelly Kloepfer points out, "the fetid sickroom over which Norah has gained control is not that space" (Kloepfer, 54). It is a cell in which she nominally rules her dependent mother, but in fact she is nurse and servant, enduring all in the hope of a small inheritance and for the praise of relatives: " 'You're wonderful, Norah'. But they did not help. They just stood around watching her youth die, and her beauty die, and her soft heart grow hard and bitter" (*ALMM*, 104).

Both the mother and younger daughter have had ambivalent feelings toward Julia: they desire to hurt her and humiliate her, but specifically in the case of Norah, they feel "more alive when . . . with her" (*ALMM*, 106). In Rhys's work, "there is always an alternation between desire and rage" (Kloepfer, 46). The desire and rage are not always directed at sexual partners or fathers, but at mothers and sisters, as well.

Gender Politics

When Mackenzie had tired of Julia he dropped her. To salve his conscience, if he had one, he did what he and his society considered "the right thing." He provided a weekly allowance sent to her through his attorneys, who threatened her not to make trouble and demanded amorous letters Mackenzie had sent her but which she had already destroyed. The money was enough for Julia to maintain herself in the room she found in which to hide and recover from the deep emotional wound the rejection had caused her. She had wanted one generous sum of money instead of the weekly dole, because then she could go away, start over in another city, or perhaps return to London and be able to subsist there for a while. But Mackenzie was not that generous. He and his lawyers seem to have planned on six months of support and then a final 1,500-franc payment to close the case. Custom and the law are on Mackenzie's side. Julia must hold her tongue if she is to survive at all. What Julia also received was "the sore and cringing feeling" that was the residue after Mackenzie departed (*ALMM*, 11).

Julia shows desperate courage in tracking Mackenzie to the restaurant, but she is not able to move him to sympathy or to rekindle the sexual feelings he must have had for her at one time. The only feeling that the confrontation engenders in him is embarrassment. In his own eyes, of course, he has behaved as a "gentleman." He had not been ungenerous and he is not rude now.

Men join ranks to protect each other from loud, raucous, and demanding women who seem to be invading the male domain of action. When Monsieur Albert, the restaurant owner, saw Julia sit down unbid at Mackenzie's table and recognized that his valued customer was discomfited, he looked at Mackenzie "with significance" (*ALMM*, 28). A male gaze is exchanged. Albert's "eyes telegraphed, 'I understand; I remember this woman. Do you want to have her put out?' " (*ALMM*, 29). Mackenzie raises an eyebrow in a haughty gaze and Albert moves away. Mackenzie has made it clear that he is in charge of the situation and there is nothing to worry about. His class and money put Albert "in his place" and indicate to all who might be observing that this wealthy man has everything under control, including the forward woman who has invaded his space and disturbed his meal.

Another male gazer in the restaurant is George Horsfield, who in a voyeuristic way becomes a party to the scene and is interested in the attractive woman. His interest is part sympathy and part desire, not an unusual combination for the dominant male. The female appears a victim in need of rescue and protective appropriation. If Julia could only have played the role of victim better, instead of merely being one, her path in life would have been easier. There is no view from Julia's perspective or any woman's perspective in the restaurant scene, for as Coral Ann Howells points out, Julia "is not a signifying subject when the male point of view governs the narrative" (Howells, 59).

James was Julia's first lover and the one she loved and respected the most. That affair "had ended quietly and decently, without fuss or scenes or hysteria" (*ALMM*, 109). He is sympathetic and kind when she visits him in London. He gives her drinks and shows her his pictures that he dearly loves, more dearly than he loves women. She thinks, "He's so damned respectable and secure. Sitting there so smugly" (*ALMM*, 112). She feels, "Because he has money he's a kind of God. Because I have none I'm a kind of worm. A worm because I've failed and I have no money. A worm because I'm not even sure if I hate you" (*ALMM*, 112–13).

James politely declines to hear of her troubles. A familiar man is little interested in a woman's narrative. The ex-lovers part with his promise to write to her. Perhaps he will continue to be her friend? But how faint is the candle flame of hope in Rhysland and how quickly it is snuffed out. When James finally does communicate with Julia, the result is devastating for her. He sends her 20 pounds and terminates the relationship: "I am afraid that after this I can do no more" (*ALMM*, 172).

James deals with Julia in the same way that Mackenzie does. Horsfield does little better. After Julia embarrasses him at her rooming house when she screams with fright in the dark on the stairs, having felt as if a corpse (her mother's body) had touched her, he begins to lose interest in her. She is too much trouble. She isn't perfect. He has slept with her so the conquest still stands, and she is not quite worth rehabilitating. He, too, ends the affair with a letter and a small check: 10 pounds (*ALMM*, 180). Although Julia is only an incident in the love lives of James, Mackenzie, and Horsfield, they are equally insignificant as individuals in her narrative, because for all practical purposes they are inter-changeable.

Characterization

The portrayal of Julia Martin is stark, startling, and vivid, depicting a woman who is a reluctant actor in her own life narrative. She is an exhausted woman, worn out not by physical work but by the depression brought on by loneliness and deep disappointments. When we first meet her in her room, "She was tired. She hardly ever thought of men, or of love" (*ALMM*, 12). Jean Rhys heroines are almost always weary, exhausted sufferers of mild to severe depression. Unconsciously, Julia resists all movement because all actions in the past have led to undesired and unexpected results: rejection, abandonment, exile. At the beginning

she has to force herself to confront Mackenzie. She is reluctant to return
to London, and when she does she loses her mother, the tentative regard
of her sister, and the man who could have helped her in her travail,
Horsfield.

The two driving forces in Julia are her love of money and her fear of
growing old. Having for many years been a kept woman, she relies upon
the will, the whims, and the generosity of her lovers for money to live on:
"It's a very easy habit to acquire" (*ALMM*, 26). But she has not been a
very skillful courtesan. She has not wheedled, haggled, and squirreled
away money for later, leaner (or heavier) times. She has been more generous with her body than her lovers have been with their money, and men
have always exercised, and continue to exercise, economic power over her.

Julia is not good with money. It is a commodity for her. When she
has some she spends it right away, especially on clothes. They make her
feel good or better, helping her to sustain some self-image as a beautiful
and desirable woman. She thinks they give her power. They are perhaps
to be considered capital investments as the tools of her trade. "She
thought of new clothes with passion, with voluptuousness. She imagined the feeling of a new dress on her body and the scent of it. And her
hands emerging from long black sleeves" (*ALMM*, 20). When she has
some money left she loses "all sense of the exact value of the money"
(*ALMM*, 19).

The money transactions between Julia and her men have as much
emotion and sexiness as making a bank deposit. When Horsfield slips
Julia a pound note, he does so with the same amount of feeling that he
expends petting his cat, and Julia takes it with even less feeling
(*ALMM*, 94). Julia goes to London for money. "This place tells you all
the time, 'Get money, get money, or be for ever damned' " (*ALMM*, 91).

Losing her looks and descending into middle age is a terror for Julia,
more of a nightmare than even her present life, for she cannot see herself
living, literally surviving, without attractiveness. The unspoken pro-
jected end for an unsuccessful demimondaine is an early death from dis-
ease and alcoholism after a brief life as a streetwalker. Julia observes a
crowd outside a cinema: "The girls were perky and pretty, but it was
strange how many of the older women looked drab and hopeless, with
timid, hunted expressions. They looked ashamed of themselves, as if
they were begging the world not to notice that they were woman or to
hold it against them" (*ALMM*, 70). An unattractive, middle-aged
woman has no right to her existence in the value system of the patriarchal world that Julia does not contest, even as Rhys does.

Drinking is aging Julia. When Horsfield says that Paris is "a difficult place for Anglo-Saxons to be sober in," Julia replies, "Oh, no place is a place to be sober in" (*ALMM*, 48). Later, in London, when drinking with Horsfield, "She looked older and less pretty than she had done in Paris. Her mouth and the lids of her eyes drooped wearily. A small blue vein under her right eye was swollen" (*ALMM*, 91). Rhys, a heavy drinker herself, has a sharp eye for such details of alcoholism as swollen facial veins. Nevertheless, "The suggestion of age and weariness in her face fascinated Mr. Horsfield. It was curious to speculate about the life of a woman like that and to wonder what she appeared to herself to be—when she looked in the glass . . . because . . . she must have some pathetic illusions about herself or she would not be able to go on living. Did she still see herself young and slim, capable of anything, believing that, though every one around her grew older, she—by some miracle— remained the same?" (*ALMM*, 91–92). Horsfield's insights are sensitive and appropriate, but he is filled with curiosity and sympathy, and not what Julia wants and needs: love, or at least enough passion for commitment.

Julia makes one final attempt in her life to exert independence. Of course it is the right move but at the wrong time. Horsfield is genuinely attempting to help her as she prepares to return to Paris. He says that he will try to visit her there or at least send her some money, but his voice is cold, although he could not help it. Julia flares up. It may be the booze talking, because "a muscle under her left eye was twitching. 'If you think . . . That I care . . . I can always get somebody, you see. I've known that ever since I've known anything' " (*ALMM*, 174).

It is a courageous moment but a victory against the wrong target. She will be putting the touch on Mackenzie again soon enough. Julia knows she has been hard on Horsfield: "She said sullenly: 'I'm sorry. You see, that's how I am' "(*ALMM*, 174). That's how she is.

Norah is the traditional daughter who has stayed close to her mother and has sacrificed much of her life to the present in the caretaking role. She is a martyr in her own eyes and in the eyes of others. Although Norah is ambivalent in her feelings for her sister Julia, both loving and hating her, Rhys portrays her with great sympathy.

Julia speaks gently to her, but Norah feels that they are always at the edge of a quarrel (*ALMM*, 102). Norah is jealous of the sexually free and adventurous life she believes Julia has lived, knowing nothing of her sister's pain and suffering. She doesn't want Julia to know of her own pain and suffering: "She did not want to give herself away before Julia—Julia

with her hateful, blackened eyelids. What was the use of telling Julia
what she thought of her? It was ridiculous to make a scene. You ignored
people like that. And yet every time she looked at Julia she felt a fierce
desire to hurt her or to see her hurt and humiliated" (*ALMM,*102). Julia
is not respectable. She is an embarrassment or even a disgrace to the
family. Even worse, she may have actually enjoyed her life and apparently has not yet been punished for it. But she is Norah's sister and
there is a blood bond between them.

At night after administering to her comatose mother, Norah thinks
of her fate: "It isn't fair. It isn't fair" (*ALMM,* 103). In the words of the
book on her bed table, Joseph Conrad's *Almayer's Folly,* she "had no hope
and knew of no change. . . . She had no wish, no hope, no love"
(*ALMM,* 103). She is a slave. She has been one for the six years of her
mother's dying. She knows that her "life's like death. It's like being
buried alive" (*ALMM,* 103). Rhys is stating sadly and profoundly that
the lives of the prodigal daughter and the good daughter who stays at
home are both miserable.

Norah cannot let Julia leave without trying to do something for her,
without an attempt at what she does well, indeed what she only does—
nurturing: "Have something to eat before you go. Bread and cheese, or
an egg, or something" (*ALMM,* 106). But Julia cannot break bread with
her sister. She does not want her nurturing. She could use her sister's
understanding and perhaps some financial help. She is after all a professional cadger. But being nurtured by her younger sister would reduce
her status and her independence even further in her own mind. Perhaps
the most tragic of the failed relationships in *After Leaving Mr. Mackenzie*
is the one between the sisters.

Upset at the funeral of her mother, Julia lashes out at her family and
its middle-class respectability and hypocrisy. She rages at them, but
Norah cannot understand rage. The gulf of understanding and experience between the sisters is too wide to bridge. It is the divide between
those who live bourgeois lives and those who dance on the far edge of
society's divide. Norah merely thinks that her sister is "disgusting, that's
what she is. She's my sister, and she's disgusting" (*ALMM,* 135). And
Julia wants to have the courage to spit in her sister's "huge, stupid face
. . . once before I die" (*ALMM,* 135). She can't act, of course, but the
desire is great. The quarrel heightens to a shouting match, and Julia is
forever cut off from her sister and the world of her childhood.

When Norah realizes that Julia is gone from her life forever, she
becomes nearly hysterical. Her love and her nurturer's feelings for Julia

reemerge: "We can't send her away like that. I don't believe she's got any money" (*ALMM*, 138). It is too late, and Norah judges herself: "My God, how hard I've got!" (*ALMM*, 139). Norah is as much the loser as is Julia. More charity and less virtue might have saved both of them.

The three lovers of Julia whom we meet in *After leaving Mr. Mackenzie* share two aspects: they are all English, and they all leave her. The text opens after the end of one affair, perhaps with an event one might call the after shock, and it ends with the conclusion of another affair. Mackenzie is comfortably well off. He made his pile and retired early. He is forty-eight years old, "of medium height and colouring. . . . He had enough nose to look important, enough stomach to look benevolent" (*ALMM*, 23). What is so special about Mackenzie (whose first name, by the way, we never learn)? Nothing. He is just one in a line of men. Arnold E. Davidson notes, "The separation is standard, predictable, part of the normal course of affairs" (Davidson, 78). What is different is that for once Julia realizes that Mackenzie's dropping her is indeed the standard outcome of her affairs, and for once she rages and strikes out in a feeble and futile rebellion.

She had thought her affairs were love affairs with the emphasis on love, and now, after six months of depression, she has awakened to realize that her romantic image of herself and her lovers was false. She has been a prostitute hired not by the hour or night but for a somewhat indefinite period of weeks or months, receiving money and gifts in exchange for sex, unstated though the bargain may have been. The men don't like to think that they are buying it. It seems too bourgeois to the bourgeoisie. They, too, need their illusions. Mackenzie is a pathetic coward and a cad. From the beginning he knew that he would eventually pay Julia off. Like Julia he is locked in a recurring pattern.

James has more class than either Mackenzie or Horsfield, but then he has more money, and presumably he had the privilege and the pleasure of being the first, the man who took Julia's virginity at 19. He was tender when he dropped her, and of course she did not make a fuss. His name for her is Julietta, as if she were a young girl in an operatic tragedy. When she calls upon him for help, her visit is tiresome for him. He thinks, "These resurrections of the past are tactless, really—not amusing. But what is one to do?" (*ALMM*, 110). The situation is giving him a headache, but he remains attentive and polite: "You've never looked prettier" (*ALMM*, 110). He gives her a drink and tells her he has "loads of time—heaps of time. Nearly three-quarters of an hour" (*ALMM*, 111). But like Mackenzie, and presumably the others, he merely wants to get rid of her. Thus he sends the ultimate, predictable letter with the final pay off and cut off.

Rhys offers little physical description of the men in the novel. It is as if Julia or she hardly sees them. They are only men. When Julia comes into the presence of her first lover, she does not recognize him. He is "simply another person," and she finds that fact "strange and sad" (*ALMM*, 110).

George Horsfield is physically described only as "a dark young man" (*ALMM*, 36), yet we come to know him best of all the men in the text. He becomes interested in Julia when he sees her rejection by Mackenzie. She is attractive and free. He begins to want to possess her, too. After all, he is in Paris, and he is there to develop and explore his sensual side. But he is a bumbler, and although he wins one night of sex with Julia, he never is able to bring himself to pursue her intensely. It is not in his nature. He cannot be sexually direct even with an experienced woman who expects men whom she has not clearly rejected to reach out to her: "He hated the feeling of intimacy" (*ALMM*, 90).

Horsfield will not pay the price of the relationship: accepting her weaknesses, her needs, her dependencies, and committing himself to deep emotional engagement and unconditional love. Sex is only an appetite. He thinks, " 'You're thirsty, drink.' It's like that. You are thirsty, and you drink. And then you wonder all sorts of things, discontentedly and disconnectedly. 'But the worst of it is,' he thought, 'that one can never know what the woman is really feeling' " (*ALMM*, 153). It may be because he is "English," as Rhys negatively perceives that nation, but Horsfield cannot consider that a woman may find it hard, perhaps impossible, to know what the man is really feeling. Julia no longer cares. Horsfield buys his way out of the aborted relationship cheaply, believing himself to have behaved gallantly, generously, and manly in the situation, but sure that Julia was not the woman to feed his masculine needs and illusions.

Julia's "lovers" represent a powerful indictment of men. They are different—rich or of modest income, compassionate or totally selfish, cultivated or crude—but always the same, at least in relations with women: exploiting, manipulative, and ultimately dedicated to self-preservation.

Narrative Technique

After Leaving Mr. Mackenzie is a novel composed in short, jerky segments, like a fragmented memory coming out of a mental fog, or like the staggering of a drunk. The short chapters within the three parts are titled with place or persons' names as if, like in *The Left Bank,* they were independent stories. The central architectonic symbol of the novel is the Fall. From the moment we meet her in her Paris hotel room to the time she says goodbye again to Mackenzie, Julia is a falling woman. The crash is immanent and inevitable. In her rapid descent Julia loses everything: her family, her husband, her child, her men, her equanimity, her mental equilibrium, her sobriety, her youth (the name *Julia* is Greek for *youthful*), her good looks, and her self-respect. She is rushing toward a personal catastrophe, but one that, through implication and extension, every woman in Western capitalist, bourgeois society is potentially capable of experiencing.

The meager and basically simple story is told from shifting perspectives. We see Julia at different times through the eyes of Mackenzie, Horsfield, James, and Norah, and we experience them through her eyes and in her memory. The subjective views reinforce the existential nature of the text. No one understands anyone else. All fail. All are really alone. Beckett replaces Descartes: we suffer therefore we are. The technique is brilliantly crafted, allowing the story to build in a modernist way to some epiphanic comprehensions. Horsfield feels safe in his escape from commitment, but he still tries to put the disturbing Julia out of his mind as he enters his house, his tiny "world of lowered voices, and of passions, like Japanese dwarf trees, suppressed for many generations. A familiar world" (*ALMM,* 175). Julia passes beyond the possibility of controlling her fate through suicide to accepting the "untidy" and black-specked life remaining her as parasite, hustler, prostitute: "It was the hour between dog and wolf, as they say" (*ALMM,* 191).

After Leaving Mr. Mackenzie is a novel about narration. Julia continually tries to tell her story: to Horsfield; to James, who will give her 45 minutes if she doesn't "harrow" him (*ALMM,* 113); to Norah; to her uncomprehending mother; even to sanctimonious Uncle Griffiths. Rhys wants to, and succeeds in, telling Julia's story, which is a woman's tale of pain and suffering not so different from her own. Perhaps Rhys is saying that women want to tell their stories so that they can explain their lives to themselves. As the narrative ends and Julia is cadging money off Mackenzie, she does not try to tell him her story. By now she knows that no one (especially men) wants to hear it. Rhys may be saying that if the woman's narrative is to really be listened to and fully understood, it would bring about some change in society's comprehension and behavior.

Imagery

The key iterative and most symbolic image of *After Leaving Mr. Mackenzie* is that of the mask. Julia had been an artist's model, posing as directed in order to fulfill someone else's imagination, and a mannequin, wearing someone else's clothes. When Horsfield picks her up in the café, the first thing she does is powder her face (*ALMM*, 40). She must put on the woman's mask. She must do what women of her time called putting on their face. Makeup will hide her blemishes, her signs of aging, and her pain. The painted mask will stay youthful and smiling until it becomes caricature. When after a movie Horsfield and Julia proceed to his room, "she sighed deeply. Then she took from her bag a small gilt powder-box and began to powder her face carefully" (*ALMM*, 46). The box is precious equipment. It contains the mask she wears in company, pretending it is her true face.

Whenever Julia has a little money, she buys new clothes. They renew her image. When Julia meets her sister again after years of estrangement, she sees that her sister's "face was cold, as though warmth and tenderness were dead in her" (*ALMM*, 71). Her reaction: "She took off her hat, powdered her face, rouged her lips" (*ALMM*, 72). Her face must not look lifeless and cold. She cannot expose her true face, her true condition, her true self to her sister in the way that her sister is willing to do with her.

When Julia and Horsfield have a date in London, "she made her inevitable, absent-minded gesture of powdering her face. She looked happier, and relieved" (*ALMM*, 90). The masking is automatic. With the mask on she is able to face the world, believing herself now attractive and thus in control of the social situation and requirements. Horsfield grows annoyed at her constant primping. He wants her to talk to him. She must be sure she is attractive before she speaks of her troubles, otherwise she might lose his attention. He says, " 'If only you'd stop worrying about how you look and tell me what's the matter.' She said: 'I thought from the way you were staring at me that I must be looking pretty ugly' " (*ALMM*, 92). Masking gets in the way of communication, and the couple have enough problems in that area without the separation of the mask.

As she views her mother's corpse, Julia sees "that her mother's sunken face, bound with white linen, looked frightening—horribly frightening, like a mask. Always masks had frightened and fascinated her" (*ALMM*, 124). Immediately outside on the street, Julia thought,

" 'I must look ghastly.' She stood under a lamp-post and powdered her face, and pulled her hat over her eyes" (*ALMM*, 125). The pose is a traditional prostitute cliché. It is not effective. She is looking for assurance that she is alive and desirable, but it does not come. At her rooming house she is met by another, presumably older woman who offers her a cup of tea and some companionship, but Julia rebuffs the friendly woman, now wanting only sleep.

After the cremation ceremony for her mother, when Julia leaves her family for the last time, having attacked them for their hypocrisy, even calling Uncle Griffiths "an abominable old man" (*ALMM*, 136), she "took out her powder and then returned it to the bag" (*ALMM*, 137). There was no need to mask now. In a sense it was too late. She had unmasked herself and her true feelings to the last of the family even as she had unmasked them. She never makes up again in the text. Perhaps she has made the archetypal journey to self-awareness.

In Jungian conceptualization the putting on of the mask is a transcending act that turns the wearer into the archetype. In *After Leaving Mr. Mackenzie* Rhys implies transformation in ironic tones, for Julia is not transformed into a symbolic young woman. As Helen Nebeker points out, "Julia's concern over her old coat and her fatness, her constant powdering of her face, her insatiable desire for new clothes reinforce this idea of woman's need to find Selfhood" (Nebeker, 18). But it is obviously the wrong way because it is the superficial way. It is an act of competition with other women for the attention of men, and it is ultimately designed for them. It is Selfhood twisted into an icon of the other sex's imagination.

In *After Leaving Mr. Mackenzie*, Rhys employs animal imagery to indicate how her heroine and perhaps many women of her generation have been dehumanized by a hostile society and turned into animals, like the bird in the wallpaper pattern in her Paris hotel room: "a large bird, sitting on the branch of a tree, faced, with open beak, a strange, wingless creature, half-bird, half-lizard, which also had its beak open and its neck stretched in a belligerent attitude" (*ALMM*, 10). The bird, perhaps as a victim to be, sits facing an apocalyptic image, a creature of nightmares. The image is a prognostication of Julia's future: a bird with a silent scream about to be devoured by a hostile society.

When Julia tries to explain to her uncle how her marriage disintegrated, he attacks her former husband, and Julia tries to defend him. Uncle Griffiths's interrogation is demeaning and dehumanizing. She shrinks from the sanctimonious barrage of rhetorical questions and unfounded conclusions: "She felt as though her real self had taken cover, as though she had retired somewhere far off and was crouching warily, like an animal, watching her body in the arm-chair arguing with Uncle Griffiths about the man she had loved" (*ALMM*, 82). Her uncle's aggression forces Julia to imagine herself as a trapped animal.

Rhys uses an animal image to show Horsfield's overwhelming need for uncomplicated relationships. After parting from Julia in a cab, saying goodnight, and pressing a pound note into her hand, he meets his cat outside his house. "When it saw him it opened and shut its mouth in a soundless mew. Mr. Horsfield said caressingly: 'Come along, Jones, Pretty Jones.' The cat got up, stretched slowly and, with uplifted tail, followed its master into the house" (*ALMM*, 94). The cat's silence and obedience are enough for Horsfield. He can be affectionate toward the cat, ostensibly a male cat, because he has complete mastery, something he knows he will never have with Julia.

Rhys and Julia's mother both understand Norah's true role as servant-daughter in the present moment of the text. Norah says to Julia, "You know she called me Dobbin the other day. And I was feeling so exactly like some poor old cart-horse when she said it" (*ALMM*, 99–100). A servant-daughter who chooses or is connived, or shamed into the final nursing of a parent is less than human. The mother, Mrs. Griffiths, leaves her human state when looking at Julia, her wayward daughter, for the last time with comprehension: "It was like seeing a spark go out and the eyes were again bloodshot, animal eyes. Nothing was there" (*ALMM*, 98).

Rejected by her family, Julia states, "Animals are better than we are, aren't they? They're not all the time pretending and lying and sneering like loathsome human beings" (*ALMM*, 135). Norah sees her sister as "an extraordinary creature" (*ALMM*, 135). Finally, Julia sums up her feelings, and perhaps Rhys's, about family and humans in general: "People are such beasts, such mean beasts. . . . do you think I'm going to cringe to a lot of mean, stupid animals?" (*ALMM*, 135).

As Julia and Horsfield proceed to her room to make love for the first and only time, Rhys describes the passing scene: "A woman in a long macintosh passed them, muttering to herself and looking mournful and lost, like a dog without a master" (*ALMM*, 145). Is this Rhys's attempt to put herself in the scene; a lonely woman, somewhat demented, forlorn, without the necessary master? It is a powerful image of future despair, prophetic for protagonist and perhaps for narrator.

The last animal image in *After Leaving Mr. Mackenzie*, previously alluded to, is most enigmatic: "Lights were beginning to come on in the cafés. It was the hour between dog and wolf, as they say" (*ALMM*, 191). The French idiom, *entre chien et loup*, refers to the point in the evening when, at twilight, it is too dark to tell the animals apart. But the twilight is Julia's as she falls toward final darkness. Furthermore, Julia is a creature between a domesticated fawning pet and the wild thing of nature that "reasonable" men believe a woman is and that makes her desirable and interesting, but requiring taming and control.

Conclusion

In this dark and despairing text the war between the sexes finds the male always winning. Julia drifts away, a battered vessel, through a series of detachments: lovers, mother, sister, uncle, and her own mind. But all are alone and drifting, all are prisoners of their senses, especially their limited sight. Loneliness is the human condition. It is in action that Rhys sees the difference between men and women. The male quest is public and dramatic, and it may result in achieving a Holy Grail. Accomplishments are the measure of its success. Puissance is the reward. The process is of little value without product. The female quest is private, predictable in process, indeterminate in results, and it ends in displacement if not self-destruction.

Alicia Borinsky points out that a woman in a Rhys text is always a guest of others, one who "serves as a minor exciting character in the lives of other characters" (Borinsky, 300). Those characters are usually men. Julia Martin is a guest who returns to haunt Mackenzie or at least disturb his digestion once in a while, but she remains in the house of our imagination. A painful implication set forth by *After Leaving Mr. Mackenzie*, and indeed endemic to Rhys's pre–World War II writing, is that women in Western civilization have lived by exploiting men while men exploit them. Women and men are antagonists. Perhaps the women's movement of the 1960s has assuaged this somewhat, at least in America. Or perhaps the tribe of women and the tribe of men have merely moved their conflict underground.

Chapter Five
Voyage in the Dark

Jean Rhys originally titled her third novel *Two Tunes,* referring to the two narrative time levels in the text: the heroine Anna Morgan's simultaneous memory of her childhood past and young adult present.[1] "Two Tunes" also symbolizes the two musical and life rhythms, Caribbean and English, that play in Anna's and Rhys's head. Just before publication Rhys wisely changed the title to *Voyage in the Dark.* The original publisher, Jonathan Cape, correctly insisted that she change the ending, to avoid lugubriousness, by allowing the heroine to survive. The novel was Rhys's only commercial success prior to *Wide Sargasso Sea.* It was very widely reviewed with praise in such publications as the *Times Literary Supplement,* the *New York Times,* the *London Sunday Times, Saturday Review, New York Herald Tribune Books,* and many others (Angier, 335, 700).

Although published in 1934 the first draft was written, rather like a therapeutic memoir, in exercise books before Rhys met Ford Madox Ford or had composed *The Left Bank* stories, *Quartet,* and *After Leaving Mr. Mackenzie* (Nebeker, 43–46; O'Connor, 57). Because of its clear autobiographical nature, Rhys, who thought very highly of *Voyage in the Dark,* was nevertheless reluctant to see the story in print, and it always pained her to look at it.

In *Voyage in the Dark* Rhys continues to tell the story of the early twentieth-century woman of no importance, who is careerless, childless, a male possession, a daughter, a lover, and a wife. *Voyage in the Dark* is the bitterly ironic story of a young, bewildered, inexperienced girl's fall (from a job in the theatrical chorus and a life lived in bleak rooming houses), through economic and sexual manipulation and control, into a life of idleness and waiting in a small room for the providing lover (with the inevitable dismissal, prostitution, pregnancy, late and almost fatal illegal abortion, and ultimate hopelessness).

This stream-of-consciousness novel is both an outstanding work of modernist fiction and a social document of significance, as it depicts the pattern of using and discarding young, unprotected, rootless women in twentieth-century Western patriarchal and bourgeois society who are programmed to look for security in life only through the largest of father-figure men skilled in seduction and control. A young woman's way is "a voyage in the dark."

Structure

Voyage in the Dark is divided into four parts. Part one, subdivided into numbered short chapters or sections, contains nearly half of the 188-page book. Anna Morgan is an 18-year-old actress and chorus dancer, born on a West Indian island. Her mother and father are dead. Her stepmother, an English woman, has brought her to England and pretty much abandoned her. Anna is an attractive young woman who has been working as a chorus girl in an English theatrical troupe. Performing in the provinces, Anna picks up an affluent stockbroker, Walter Jeffries, who is nearly 20 years older. He is taken with her and arranges to meet her in London, where on a dinner date he takes her to a posh men's club to dine in a private room with an accompanying bedroom. From the beginning of their relationship, Walter plies Anna with drink. They consume two bottles of wine and have after-dinner cordials, perhaps starting the 18-year-old on the road to debilitating alcohol dependency. Jeffries makes his crude move, but Anna rejects him. He recovers his manners and, considering that she is worth some effort, he behaves more considerately. Anna is attracted to him. He has power, money, savoir faire, and is a potential father figure for the orphan girl. Before they can date again, Anna becomes ill, as she often does in times of stress (which is almost always), and Jeffries appears with food, uses his power to intimidate the mean-spirited landlady, and provides a doctor for the girl. At last someone in England is taking care of Anna, a status that she, and most Rhys heroines, greatly desires. Anna and Walter continue to date, and although Anna recognizes Walter's prurience, she goes to bed with him willingly, for she has fallen in love with him.

As an alien to British culture, poor Anna never understands that men of Jeffries's class have a rigid, class-defined attitude to women of the working class, Anna's present status, although she was born into a privileged colonial class. Those men marry only women of their own class for the protection and control of property, but they enjoy sex with working-class women over whom they exercise economic control.

During the progress of her involvement with Jeffries, Anna recalls and dreams of her childhood on her island, comparing her earlier life in a lush if imperfect Eden, surrounded by people like her father, whom she loved and who loved her, with her cold existence in England, with no

loving person except, as she deludes herself into believing, Walter Jeffries. Feeling guilt and fear over her affair, Anna visits with her stepmother Hester, seeking guidance and counsel, but the older woman is
only interested in complaining about her in-laws back on the island and
making it clear to Anna that she will not provide her with any financial
support.

Hester suspects that her stepdaughter is receiving money from a
man, but she does not wish to acknowledge it for fear that an alteration
in Anna's status might involve a financial obligation for her. As
expected, Jeffries tires of Anna, and in a cowardly fashion drops her by
having his unctuous younger cousin, Vincent, another womanizer, write
to her and handle the breakup in a way that is least disturbing to Walter. Through the promise of financial aid, Vincent secures Anna's assurance that she will not cause trouble for his cousin. But neither Walter
nor Victor have considered or understood her inexperience and fragile
mental state. Anna goes to pieces.

Parts two and three are each about half as long as part one, and each
is also divided into brief, numbered chapters or sections. In part two
Anna, now 19, tries to assuage her pain. She tries to understand herself
and what has happened to her by reaching out to an older woman, Ethel
Matthews, a possible mother surrogate for her but in fact a woman of
low character who facilitates Anna's slide into selective prostitution.

In part three Anna, who has been drinking heavily and is living in
Ethel's flat, ineptly attempts to eke out a living as a manicurist. She
spends much of her time recollecting her happier life as a child on her
island and her earlier days in England, when she was touring in musicals
and had not met Jeffries. She takes a new paying lover, a married American gambler named Carl Redman, who is more crass than Jeffries but
more honest and direct. Anna generously, but foolishly, "lends" a por-
tion of the money she has saved to one of her chorus friends. Carl leaves
and Anna begins to pick up johns and bring them to her room. Soon she
is pregnant and living with her friend, with no idea as to who the father
is: " 'It was that one I went back with just after Carl left.' Counting back
and thinking. 'No, I don't think it was that time. I think it was when
. . .' " [the ellipse is Rhys's].[2] When Anna is ill she dreams of her lost
island and the sea. She writes to Walter for help, and Vincent shows up
to provide the forty pounds needed for an illegal abortion. Anna is
required to turn over to Vincent any letters she has from Walter. Part
three ends with Anna having her abortion at the hands of a Mrs. Robinson. Injured, she returns to Laurie's flat.

Part four is a one-chapter, five-page epilogue. Anna is in bed, drinking and in a semiconscious state, having flashbacks of sex with an older man and carnival memories of Blacks and Whites in reverie. She is in need of a physician, who must be told a lie to cover the abortion. She had dreamt of falling: "I fell for a hell of a long time then." Her friend says, "That's right. . . . When he comes tell him that" (V, 187). Anna has fallen indeed. When conscious again she hears the doctor saying, "You girls are too naïve to live, aren't you?" (V, 187). The final lines of dialogue in the text are also the doctor's: " 'She'll be all right,' he said. 'Ready to start all over again in no time, I've no doubt' " (V, 187).

The doctor's words are devastatingly ironic—start all over again at what? another, better, and happier life? or another tour of street walking, pregnancy, and abortion? Regardless of what the doctor means, Rhys is unambiguous. Anna thinks "about being new and fresh . . . when anything might happen. And about starting all over again, all over again" (V, 188). But Anna's lot in life will not improve despite her desire to be "new and fresh." Joe Adler, Carl's sycophant, has told her "Nobody wins. Don't worry. Nobody wins" (V, 155). Starting all over means doing it again the same way. How she wishes that her drama could be different. As the curtain drops on the sad life of a chorus girl, she is still falling. Does Anna Morgan become Julia Martin?

A Post-Colonial Caribbean Text

Related to the social document aspect of the novel, noted above, *Voyage in the Dark,* like *Wide Sargasso Sea,* is also a work of post-colonial Caribbean literature. Anna is a West Indian immigrant to England torn between a culture presently experienced and one happily remembered (Howells, 69). Young Anna is making a perilous voyage in her 18th through 20th years, out of adolescence into womanhood, out of the small bright island of Dominica (never specifically mentioned but established by longitude and latitude) into dark and dangerous England, and in the present tense of the novel she is at sea in darkest, exploiting, capitalist, patriarchal England without one or more pilots, such as a caring mother or father or a community of more experienced, concerned women.

As stated previously, *Voyage in the Dark* was originally titled *Two Tunes,* a title reflecting the two cultures that intertwine within Anna's English and white Creole (Black-French-Welsh-English) sensibilities. In *Voyage in the Dark* the West Indian subtextuality seen in *The Left Bank,*

Quartet, and *After Leaving Mr. Mackenzie* surfaces, and Anna's Caribbean
background and ongoing recollections confirm Rhys's identity as a
Caribbean writer if not a contributor to Caribbean culture. A fuller contribution by Rhys to a Caribbean canon is found, of course, in *Wide Sargasso Sea.*
      Anna's thoughts and memories provide the West Indian content of
the text as well as the poetic quality of the prose. Anna is informed
about West Indian history, particularly concerning her native island. A
sentimental music hall song triggers a textbook-like memory.

> The Caribs indigenous to this island were a warlike tribe and their resis-
> tance to white domination, though spasmodic, was fierce. As lately as the
> beginning of the nineteenth century they raided one of the neighbouring
> islands, under British rule, overpowered the garrison and kidnapped the
> governor, his wife and three children. They are now practically extermi-
> nated. The few hundred that are left do not intermarry with the negroes.
> Their reservation, at the northern end of the island, is known as the Carib
> Quarter. They had . . . a king, Mopo, his name was. Here's to Mopo,
> King of the Caribs! (*V*, 105)

The novel begins with Anna closing her eyes, putting cold and
frightening England out of her mind, and pretending she is "home" on
her island, "looking down Market Street to the Bay. When there was a
breeze the sea was millions of spangles; and on still days it was purple as
Tyre and Sidon" (*V*, 7). The colors of home, even in memory, are vivid for
Anna, while England is always gray, drab, and pale like its people.
      In one of Rhys's most brilliant prose passages, Anna recalls a first
panorama of England, when at the age of 16, newly arrived from the
West Indies and on a train with her stepmother, she views her new
country.

> This is England Hester said and I watched it through the train window
> divided into squares like pocket-handkerchiefs; a small tidy look it had
> everywhere fenced off from everywhere else—what are those things—
> those are haystacks—oh are those haystacks—I had read about England
> ever since I could read—smaller meaner everything is never mind—this
> is London—hundreds thousands of white people white people rushing
> along and the dark houses all alike frowning down one after the other all
> alike all stuck together—the streets like smooth shut-in ravines and the
> dark houses frowning down—oh I'm not going to like this place I'm not
> going to like this place I'm not going to like this place—you'll get used

to it Hester kept saying I expect you feel like a fish out of water but
you'll soon get used to it. (*V,* 17)

This stream-of-consciousness passage is reminiscent of the 1930s
poetry of W. H. Auden and Stephen Spender, with its evocation of the
rhythm of a moving train, the rushing-by sights of a journey through
the English countryside, and the arrival in London. At the same time the
description portrays the young girl's amazement at the sight of things
only read about, a developing fear and sense of confinement in a place so
orderly and fenced off, and her conviction stated in coordination with
the steady strokes of the engine piston, "I'm not going to like this
place."

Anna and Rhys's descriptions of places on her island and on the
great, confusing Island of Britain differ vastly in feeling, and that difference is of great significance to *Voyage in the Dark.* Louis James notes,
"When Jean Rhys recreates the West Indian house with its verandah
and latticed jalousies, dazed by the sun at noon, haunted by the moon at
night, the prose itself becomes luminous. We see through the eyes of a
child, reacting with responses of wonder."[3]

But the English landscape is painted without sensuousness. It is an
ordinary, monotonous, uninspiring place of pocket handkerchief squares
of land well fenced off. The sky and the smoke are the same color. As
Anna falls under the power of Jeffries and in effect becomes his economic
and sexual slave, without of course the tenure of actual, legal slavery, she
echoes, in accidental irony, her stepmother's words: "Of course, you get
used to things, you get used to anything" (*V,* 40). One can get used to
slavery but still ask, "My God, how did this happen?" (*V,* 40).

On the other hand Anna masochistically says of her sexual servility,
"But I like it like this. I don't want it any other way but this" (*V,* 56).
Anna's loss of freedom accompanied by Jeffries's caretaking brings to
her imagining conscious mind feelings of guilt over her White family's
historical participation in slavery and her own childhood identification
with Black people. Anna recalls seeing an "old slave-list at Constance"
(*V,* 52), the ancient family estate, and she has never forgotten the names
on the list, as if trying in her memory to give those people a human existence denied to them in their lives: "Maillote Boyd, aged 18, mulatto,
house servant" (*V,* 53). Significantly, she continues, "The sins of the
fathers . . . are visited upon the children unto the third and fourth generation" (*V,* 53). Anna is the fifth generation. When she is in bed with
Walter, the name Maillote Boyd, like her a slave age 18, comes to mind

again and ties her slavery to his, linking her guilt over her illicit sexual relationship and the pleasure it brings with historical guilt.

Anna misses the Black nurse and servant Francine, whom she both loved and hated, but who nursed her through the tropical fever she contracted when she was a child, and which still afflicts her. "I always wanted to be black. I was happy because Francine was there. . . . Being black is warm and gay, being white is cold and sad" (*V*, 31).

It was Francine who explained the onset of her first menstrual period in a way that assuaged alarm and made it seem natural. When Anna discussed it with her stepmother, however, she felt miserable and wanted to die (*V*, 68). As a child Anna understood Black—White antagonism: "But I knew that of course she [Francine] disliked me too because I was white; and that I would never be able to explain to her that I hated being white. Being white and getting like Hester" (*V*, 72). The menarche in the Black world of the Islands meant an initiation into the power and the pleasure of womanhood; in the wide White world it was an "initiation into aging, sadness, loss and death, and worst of all, isolation" (O'Connor, 95).

Anna's dreams and recollections of her island past culminate in part four, after her abortion, when she remembers seeing a white mask with the face of an idiot at an island carnival masquerade, in which Whites watch Black reverie and make derisive remarks, but at which the child Anna was fascinated and frightened by the laughing Blacks (*V*, 184–87).

The feverish Anna, who takes the only drug she knows for her postpartum fever, quinine, both associates and represses her ordeal in the abortion and in the doctor's gynecological examination by recalling a horseback ride through the Black carnival. The ride made her sick, while the world seemed green and smelled of cooking fish (*V*, 186). "I tried to hang back but it was useless and the next moment my feet were groping for the stirrups——there weren't any stirrups—I balanced myself in the saddle trying to grip with my knees" (*V*, 186). As the novel ends, Anna seems to be living in the English present and the Dominican past simultaneously. The island "tune" is as vibrant and central to Rhys's narrative as the English "tune."

Themes

Exile

Exile is the great theme of *Voyage in the Dark,* the exile of Anna Morgan, who has been taken over the sea in a White reversal of the Middle Pas-

sage, and, as originally conceived by Rhys, who voyages into the ultimate and darkest exile: death. The locale of Anna's exile and indeed her
place of torment is cold, drab, business-driven, aggressive England,
where the appearance of class mobility, especially for the young and
attractive, hides the predation of the rich. The island was warm, comforting, friendly, colorful, and firmly hierarchical in social stratification.
There she was indulged as part of an ascendancy: the White planters.
She was educated in a convent school and brought up as a cosseted and
traditionally feminine young woman, not expected or expecting to earn
her own living, but to be protected by the affluent and strong.

One small insight, highly symbolic, into Anna's constructive helplessness occurs when her friend Laurie wants her to go out on a double
date, but Anna says, "I can't come in this dress. It's torn under the arm
and awfully creased" (V, 117). It does not seem to occur to her that with
a needle and thread she could sew the dress, and with an iron, perhaps
borrowed from the landlady and heated in the kitchen, she could press
her dress. She does not entertain that action because on the island that
work was done by Black servants for White women.

Anna is a romantic, idealistic young person in a strange country who
is almost totally without the resources to make her own way and protect
herself from sexual and economic exploitation. She is a Viola in an Illyria
without courtesy. Indeed Rhys goes so far as to imply that whereas Anna
has been brought up with the knowledge of how to mix drinks well for
company, she has not been well prepared, despite her religious education, to defy immorality, and the primary reason for that fact is the
absence of engaged parents. Her mother and father are dead, and her
stepmother is only interested in her own economic welfare.

The year is 1914 and very few women are in the work force, at least
until war requires their work effort. With her limited education Anna
can do little but clerk in a shop, as women were not present in the
industrial work force in any substantial numbers. Typing was not yet
woman's work. Shop clerks and servant girls were as subject to sexual
exploitation as were chorus girls. One way or another Anna has only her
youth and beauty to sell, lured to trade on them by the glitz of the theater that masked its grim reality, and finally to accept the deceptively
easier life of a demimondaine, in which she could be subjected to arbi-
trary examinations by medical and police authorities under the infamous
Contagious Diseases Acts (Emery, 96).

Anna has been exiled from her colonist class to the working class, and
her trade is semiskilled, hazardous, prone to a biological consequence,
and usually short-lived. In the end every place, person, and institution

has failed the exile Anna Morgan: England, religion, society, heterosexual comity, family, friendship, and even her island, for it did not prepare her well for life beyond its narrow limits.

The Loss of Mother

Anna Morgan is a child-woman. Like a female child in a fairy tale, she has been given into the "care" of the false mother, the evil or uncaring stepmother. Hester is the voice of England, the land of misogyny. Hester has "an English lady's voice with a sharp, cutting edge to it. Now that I've spoken you can hear that I'm a lady. I have spoken and I suppose you now realize that I'm an English gentlewoman. I have my doubts about you. Speak up and I will place you at once. Speak up, for I fear the worst. That sort of voice" (V, 57).

That voice, especially to a girl with a telltale trace of a West Indian accent, is not a comforting one. It is forbidding, censoriously matriarchal and yet simultaneously patriarchal in its reinforcement of class power through dialect. It is an "I" voice speaking a discourse of separation, not of caring communication. Deborah Kelly Kloepfer says, "It is Hester's language that severs her from any kind of relationship with Anna" (Kloepfer, 67). The mother tongue, the (m)other language, the words of caring, loving, and teaching self-preservation are forever lost to Anna.

But if Anna's mother's words are lost, the images of her maternal island home are vivid in her mind along with the names of flowers and trees. The mother island speaks to Anna of sensuality but not, in its Eden-like projection of innocence, of caution and control. To replace the useless stepmother, Anna creates a surrogate mother to relate to in her troubled thoughts: the Black nurse, servant Francine, who is discussed below.

Money

The need for, the desire for, and the great power of money in Rhys's works continues thematically and architectonically in *Voyage in the Dark*. Anna's stepmother and other members of her family abandon her because they don't want to spend their money helping her. Jeffries's great power over Anna, and Redman's, too, is due to their money. Rhys implies that everything in English society is for sale: sex, love, beauty in the form of clothes and makeup, comfort, friendship, and even abortion.

Within this society women are very cheap. One of the most damning indictments of English life in the pre–World War I period occurs when

Anna's friend Maudie relates some comments a man addressed to her: "It's funny, he said, have you ever thought that a girl's clothes cost more than the girl inside them? . . . Well, it's true, isn't it? You can get a very nice girl for five pounds, a very nice girl indeed; you can even get a very nice girl for nothing if you know how to go about it. But you can't get a very nice costume for her for five pounds. To say nothing of underclothes, shoes . . ." (*V*, 45–46). Maudie believes it is true: "People are much cheaper than things. . . . Some dogs are more expensive than people, aren't they?" (*V*, 46). Anna's understated response is merely to say, "I don't like London. It's an awful place" (*V*, 46). And the obtuse Maudie thinks her friend is a little crazy: "Whoever heard of anybody who didn't like London?" (*V*, 46).

Alcohol Abuse

Early in the text Anna and her house mate Maudie pick up Walter Jeffries and his friend and bring them to their rooming house after the men buy two bottles of port. Thus Anna and Walter's relationship starts with drinking (*V*, 11–13). When Jeffries makes his first assault, a sophisticated attempt at seducing Anna by bringing her to a private room with an attached bedroom at a private club, he makes sure she has much to drink. They have two bottles of wine and then liqueurs. Jeffries makes his move and begins to kiss Anna, but the 18-year-old has had a bit too much to drink. As this nearly middle-aged man is kissing her, she "was thinking about the man at that supper-party at the Greyhound, Croydon" (*V*, 22).

Jeffries, egotistical and self-assured, assumes that her lack of enthusiasm for sex is due to her inexperience: "You don't know how to kiss. I'll show you how to kiss. This is what you do" (*V*, 22). But Anna is giddy from drink, and, perhaps thinking of leaving the room, she accidentally opens the door to the bedroom, the existence of which she was unaware. He grabs her and she pushes him away violently: "Damn you, let me go. Damn you. Or I'll make a hell of a row" (*V*, 23). Jeffries, a proper English gentleman, does not, of course, want to be a part of a "scene" and wisely backs off, willing to bide his time until the next opportunity arises, confident that he will eventually succeed. And indeed, as Anna is resting alone on the bed, she wishes that the wealthy father-figure would return and make love to her "differently"—romantically, lovingly.

Anna becomes Jeffries's mistress after he has shown fatherly concern for her when she is ill. He takes her to a posh restaurant, and, after eating and drinking, they go out on the street to find a taxi, and everything in sight is distorted in Anna's eyes, "as if I were drunk" (*V*, 35). She finally goes to bed with Jeffries. It is a half-hearted act on her behalf. She is bewildered, befuddled, unsure, looking for the door to leave and saying, "I must go, I must go," (*V*, 37) as she is being led up the stairs to his bedroom.

As time passes Anna no longer wants the lighter alcoholic drinks. When Jeffries says, "Be happy. I want you to be happy," her reply is to ask for the drug: "All right, I'll have a whisky. . . . No, not wine—whisky." Jeffries is somewhat surprised and perhaps a little gratified that another dependency has been effected: "You've learnt to like whisky already, haven't you?"

She has, but it is not so surprising, for she comes from a culture and a family where liquor is the social lubricant and where as a child she learned to "mix a good punch" (*V*, 51). Anna understands her dependency, even if she is unaware of its consequences: "It's in my blood . . . All my family drink too much" (*V*, 51). As he is leading Anna to his bed once more, Jeffries sardonically comments, "Champagne and whisky is a great mixture" (*V*, 55). Great for the seducer, that is.

When as Jeffries's mistress she has sad thoughts about the possible outcome of the relationship, Anna assuages them by drinking (*V*, 74–75), and after Jeffries jilts her, Anna's subsequent seductions are always preceded by heavy drinking, with Anna sometimes undressed and brought to bed without fully realizing what is happening to her (*V*, 118, 122–28). By the time she has her difficult abortion and is suffering in the recovery period, she needs gin to alleviate the pain and take her out of her unhappy self (*V*, 184).

Part of the extended cautionary tale that is the Rhys canon concerns the use and misuse of alcohol. Rhys implies that one of the dangers women face in society is addiction to alcohol at the cost of their intuitive defenses and rational control of sexual situations. And for men, alcohol is a tool of seduction and a stimulant for aggressive sexual behavior if not performance.

Women against Women

In Anna's perception and experience, women are almost as much her antagonists as men are: the rooming house landladies who despise her, the foolish fellow chorus girls who encourage the younger girl into concubinage, Ethel, the older woman who tries to manipulate Anna into prostitution. A sardonic male voice for once speaks for Rhys when the slimy sycophant Joe Adler says to Anna and her friend Laurie when they are putting down another woman at a nearby restaurant table, "Oh women. How you love each other, don't you?" (*V*, 119). It is sad how Rhys depicts a woman's isolation. Even when Anna is in a theatrical company and has some friendship and support, it is fleeting. When the other chorus girls individually relate to Anna, they take advantage of her innocence and inexperience or they give her bad advice. Almost all of Rhys's minor female characters seem selfish, venal, and co-opted by the dominant patriarchal culture. Where is there another woman to like and to trust?

Characterization

"Anna is an archetypal Jean Rhys heroine" (Angier, 314). She is an attractive woman, more passive than active, who loves pleasure but seldom considers the ultimate consequences of her action or lack of action in pursuit of comfort and security, during which she often takes the line of least resistance. She is dreamy, moody, and mercurial in her mood shifts. When trapped or in despair, she does not think rationally but reacts recklessly. She has been abandoned by her family. She is an exile and basically alone. She has no brakes. She cannot stop the voyage in and into the dark. Clearly, as Pearl Hochstadt points out, "The Jean Rhys heroine is not Everywoman."[4]

Elizabeth Abel makes a very strong case for seeing Anna, who is apathetic, passive, erratic, and convinced that the world is gray and life is flat, as a sufferer from schizophrenia.[5] Anna is a person of fragmented voices. She projects two existences simultaneously: the mechanical outer self, a false self that is associated with her body and that minimally comprehends reality; and a retreating inner self, a seemingly truer self that is split off from the mechanical self and that lives more happily in her childhood past on her island. Yet as first person narrator of her life, Anna is yet a third self ineffectually interacting with either the mechanical or inner self. Thus Anna, the "author" of her life, creates a "collage of outer and inner experience"[6] made up of her humiliations, degradation, memory, and a degree of madness.

Anna is woman as victim and loser. She is even a subject of ridicule to her lover, his cousin Vincent, and Vincent's French girlfriend Germaine, who says in Anna's presence "she looks about sixteen" (*V*, 85). Vincent says, "Dear old Walter . . . has been doing a bit of baby-snatching, I'm afraid" (*V*, 85). They want to know how she and Walter met, and she ingenuously indicates that she was a showgirl and he picked her up in "Southsea." They laugh. Walter enters and is chagrined that Anna has revealed that he was out hunting for a girl on a Southsea pier. But soon he is laughing at her, too. She protests, "Oh, stop laughing at me. I'm sick of it. . . . What's the joke?" (*V*, 86). They keep on laughing at her. She is beneath them, she is excluded from the group by being made the subject of the joke, and she is denied language and the right of verbal response because of Walter and Vincent's assumed upper-class positions. Without facile access to words, Anna gives Walter a little of what he deserves when in anger, frustration, and exasperation she jams the lighted end of her cigarette down on Walter's hand (*V*, 86). Anna has her moments. Anna Morgan is one of Rhys's finest creations: a haunting, pathetic, but somehow endearing character not easily forgotten.

Walter Jeffries, a man of business, knows the price a girl like Anna will command: a few good times, some spending money for clothes, an allowance for a cheap room, and "the semblance of a romantic interest" (Davidson, 52). He is willing to pay the price. It is cheap for him. His ultimate victory is escaping from marriage or a long-term commitment and responsibility; when he is tired of a girl, he can go on to the next conquest, while the discarded young woman is passed down the line of men, each of whom will treat her more brutally.

Jean Rhys's dislike of England and need to vilify English men, in characters like Heidler, Mackenzie, and Jeffries, were motivated by displaced anger and a sense of shame at having been taken advantage of, sexually used, and betrayed by at least two English "gentlemen": her first lover, Lancelot Smith, when she was a young girl; and her first mentor, Ford Madox Ford.

Hester Morgan is a woman totally determined to have the best life she can for herself, and that includes not having any responsibility for another woman's daughter. She is a Victorian, at home in the patriarchal country of her birth and partly alienated from her stepdaughter because the girl is a child of the hot, exotic, sexually permissive island she had to live on until her husband died and she could rush home, sell the property he left her, and spend her life in genteel English surroundings. She also shows her hypocritical Victorianism in that as long as she does not have to help support her stepdaughter, she is willing to overlook the fact that Anna is leading an immoral and dangerous life. What isn't spoken or acknowledged isn't happening.

Ethel Matthews is the older woman Anna may become if she hardens, desensitizes, and survives. Ethel is blowsy, conniving, overweight, middle-aged, alcoholic, and clearly a survivor. She goes into business as a "masseuse," although she claims to have trained as a nurse. Even thought she believes men to be "brutes and idiots," she makes her living off them either as a procurer or a hooker herself when she can get clients. She talks Anna into renting one of her rooms and takes her money while trying to lure her into prostitution under the guise of teaching her young novice the trade of manicurist. Ethel is no surrogate mother to Anna but one of her exploiters. It is under Ethel's pressure that Anna becomes an out-and-out prostitute. There is something very Dickensian in Rhys's broad-brushed creation of Anna's older woman "friend."

Francine is the surrogate mother of Anna's memory. (Anna's mother may have been "coloured"; see *V*, 65.) She is a sensual woman, who nursed Anna when she was ill with fever, who cooked good food, and who taught her about menstruation. Francine is Anna's role model for a woman's life of purpose and joy. Anna recalls, "The thing about Francine was that when I was with her I was happy. She was small and plump and blacker than most of the people out there, and she had a pretty face. What I liked was watching her eat mangoes. Her teeth would bite into the mango and her lips fasten on either side of it, and while she sucked you saw that she was perfectly happy" (*V*, 67–68). Anna would like to be Black, for Francine is also an alter ego for Anna, a woman whose libido is free of religious and middle-class social guilt and hypocrisy.

The major characters in *Voyage in the Dark* are few but finely drawn. Besides functioning in the simple but well-crafted plot, each carries a symbolic burden as representative of gender, class, race, age, and a moral position.

Narrative Technique

The story of *Voyage in the Dark* comes to us directly through the fragmented voice of Anna, which reflects her confusion, depression, suffering, and pain. The voice shifts from present to past modes, sometimes from chapter to chapter, passage to passage, or even sentence to sentence. The text slips easily and skillfully back and forth through time. The effect is a well-crafted interior monologue, a stream-of-consciousness tapestry woven with people's voices, experiences, feelings, memories, colors, and sensations depicting the conscious and unconscious levels of Anna's mind.

The economy of the text is remarkable. Rhys seems to have pared it to just enough. Carole Angier observes that Rhys "always stuck close to what she could do, and avoided what she couldn't: it was an advantage of her intensity and narrowness that she almost couldn't do otherwise. But nowhere is this more true than in *Voyage*" (Angier, 299).

Imagery

Voyage in the Dark is replete with image chains that symbolize and parallel Anna's fate. The image patterns are an objective correlative to Anna's perceptions and desires.[7] Because Anna's unconscious mind feels that she is confined as an alien in an unfriendly country (a hostile, male-dominated society) and an impoverished condition, it seems clear that the most significant iterative thematic image is that of confinement, primarily manifested in the text by images of and references to rooms.

The rooms in the boarding houses that the chorus girls lodge in from town to town are essentially the same. In the one at the beginning of the novel, "There was a glass door behind the sofa. You could see into a small, unfurnished room, and then another glass door led into the walled-in garden" (*V*, 9). "The walled-in garden emblemizes Rhys's perception of English Society" (Curtis, 155). Small rooms and even the garden are walled in, as opposed to the large house Anna lived in on her island and the open countryside that she could wander freely in as child and youth.

Jeffries's first attempt at seducing Anna is in a private dining room, and when she retreats from him it is into an inner room, the cold bedroom where "the lights were shaded in red" (*V*, 23). When she returns to her "little room . . . it had a cold, close smell. It was like being in a small, dark box" (*V*, 24–25). The image is both a prison image and a death image; the cold, ill-smelling box is like a coffin. Outside, the house is surrounded by "spiked iron railings" (*V*, 34).

When Anna recalls one of many episodes of illness, this time in Newcastle, she thinks about "the room I had there, and that story about the walls of a room getting smaller until they crush you to death" (*V*, 30). Even before the story's present, Anna felt the world closing in on her. Significantly, she is referring to Edgar Allan Poe's horror story "The Pit and the Pendulum." For Anna her life is a horror story, too: fiery walls are closing in on her, also, and pushing her into the pit.

The best and worst moments of Anna's affair with Jeffries take place in the bedrooms in which they make love, and when he abandons her, she punishes herself with days alone in her own room. As Anna rides in a

taxi to a postscript of a meeting with Jeffries, she remembers a flat
where "there were three flights of stairs and then a small room and it
smelt musty" (*V*, 96). Anna knows that her rendezvous with Jeffries will
not release her from her misery. In her room she "can sleep as if I were
dead" (*V*, 113).

It is in a small, cold hotel room without a lock on the door that Joe
tries to take advantage of Anna when she lies drunk (*V*, 126–27). The
room in which Anna finally begins to take tricks starts out, in Ethel's
words, as "a lovely room" (*V*, 133). As Anna sinks lower she starts
"thinking of all the bedrooms I had slept in and how exactly alike they
were . . . Always a high, dark wardrobe and something dirty red in the
room" (*V*, 150). Dried blood? And of course it is in a bedroom in Mrs.
Robinson's flat where Anna has her abortion (*V*, 176). In post abortion
pain at her friend Laurie's flat, Anna finds the room is "nearly dark" (*V*,
183) as she nears the end of her fall and the narrative concludes.

Water images in *Voyage in the Dark* and elsewhere in the Rhys canon
signify drowning and a wish for death. When Anna learns that Walter
no longer wants to make love to her, she feels that, "It was like letting
go and falling back into water and seeing yourself grinning up through
the water, your face like a mask, and seeing the bubbles coming up as if
you were trying to speak from under the water. And how do you know
what it's like to try to speak from under water when you're drowned?"
(*V*, 98). Like Hamlet, Anna desires death but fears the possibility and
pain of a life afterward.

Later, when trying to throw Anna out of her flat, Ethel says, "Why
don't you clear out?" Anna replies, "I can't swim well enough, that's one
reason" (*V*, 145). Having to leave her miserable existence with Ethel is
for Anna like being forced into the drowning that is life on the streets,
and she knows she cannot long survive there.

Pregnant, broke, and desperate, Anna dreams that she is on a ship
approaching an island, and that she tries to catch a tree branch and step
ashore, but the tree is an English tree and it fails her as the ship's deck
expands. Someone falls overboard. We assume it is Anna. The next
image is that of "a sailor carrying a child's coffin" (*V*, 165). The passage
is proleptic. The dead child is the embryo she is shortly to abort, and it
is child Anna herself, whose life in England has lost its meaning and
value to her. She cannot reach her island or return to her happier, secure
childhood.

The last iterative, thematic image I shall discuss is the animal image,
although there are other architectonic image chains in the text. Rhys

chooses insects, small vulnerable animals, predators, and slavish pets as her menagerie: animal victims, or dangerous or disgusting beasts and fish. The chorus girls' hostel is called the "Cats' House," and the praying matron has a "little, short nose and . . . long moving lips. Just like a rabbit . . . a blind rabbit" (*V*, 21). Anna, who thinks "there's something horrible about any sort of praying," sees the praying matron as a dumb, blind, vulnerable animal.

Anna observes people without money swarming "like woodlice when you push a stick into a woodlice-nest at home." And their faces are the color of woodlice (*V*, 26). She is very afraid that she has become an insect, like the masses. On her island, too, the faces of the White people are like "woodlice" (*V*, 54).

When Anna dreams of her Uncle Bo, the parsimonious relative who had refused to help Anna financially, she imagines that "long yellow tusks like fangs came out of his mouth and protruded down to his chin" (*V*, 92). Uncle Bo is a monster, a predatory boar to her.

Ethel Matthews, who tries to feed off Anna, is described as a cunning insect with feelers and claws (*V*, 107). When Anna is in Ethel's clutches, she envisions trees as "spiders, and others like octopuses" (*V*, 142). Anna often resorts to symbolic action in place of the words she does not possess or, in her patriarchal environment, she has no right to, as when Anna manifests her disgust with her life as a prostitute by destroying a hated picture of a dog in the room she rents from Ethel. The picture over her bed is called "*Loyal Heart*," and it shows a dog sitting up begging (*V*, 148). Anna hates dogs anyway (*V*, 71). She exclaims, "I can't stand that damned dog any longer," and she throws her shoe at the picture, smashing the glass (*V*, 161). Symbolically, she is trying to destroy the image of herself as a begging pet with a heart loyal to sexual slavery. Ironically, she immediately becomes sick to her stomach and realizes she is pregnant. That is what a loyal heart and living off men has brought her.

Rhys's use of thematic imagery in *Voyage in the Dark* is part of her fine literary skills. Anna's fears, disgusts, views of people, knowledge of her victimization, and anticipation of loss and pain are indirectly stated by linking images that Rhys uses structurally as a poet does.

Conclusion

Voyage in the Dark is a powerful personal expression of a great artist's rendering of a period of her own history. It has what Elaine Showalter calls "female content" and "female style,"[8] the former because it is obviously a woman's story, and the latter because it addresses women as its primary audience, while speaking the language of female experience, often not in purely denotative words but in imagery of emotion, endurance, and swift reactions.

Rhys's text is often hard on women, as if to blame the victims for their sufferings, but that fact is related to one of *Voyage in the Dark*'s great virtues: it is never sentimental. I would find it hard to disagree with Carole Angier's summation: "*Voyage in the Dark* is the most beautifully written of all the novels, with the exception of Part One of *Wide Sargasso Sea*" (Angier, 313).

Chapter Six
Good Morning, Midnight

In *Good Morning, Midnight* the Jean Rhys heroine has grown older, has returned to Paris, and is down and out in that city once more. It is October 1937, the depths of the Depression, and terrible things are happening as the world moves toward the war that will break out almost simultaneously with the publication of *Good Morning, Midnight* in 1939. Ironically, at that time Europe was about to say good morning to midnight as the Germans and the Italians devalued humanity and prepared to end democracy in the West. But Rhys is not interested in current events. Her world remains the places inside a woman's mind and heart. Yet the heroine of *Good Morning, Midnight*, Sasha Jansen, unlike such Virginia Woolf heroines as Mrs. Dalloway and Mrs. Ramsey, must make her way in the real world, a place where hardly anyone unselfishly cares about those who are in pain or in despair.

The story of Sasha Jansen's sufferings is simultaneously one person's narrative and "a representative fable."[1] Sasha is a failure. She has failed as wife, lover, mother, and worker. And she is well aware of her imperfections. She makes no excuses, and Rhys has none for her either. She is a woman past 40 who is sure that her best years have past. She desires death but has failed in her attempt to commit suicide. Instead she sets out to kill herself with alcohol, using a small financial inheritance to bring about this end. Having used up most of her money without dying, she is given some more by an old friend, not for the purpose of self-destruction but to get to Paris and to start life over again.

With drink and depression her mind drifts in and out of the present and the past. We learn that Sasha once worked in Paris and lost her job and that she met Enno Jansen in London and married him in Amsterdam. They made their way to Paris by borrowing from friends. There they were terribly poor and insecure. Enno grew dissatisfied with Sasha and left her expecting a child. A son was born with the aid of a midwife but died at birth. Sasha failed at jobs in Paris and returned to live in London. That is her simple and sad story until the present, when she has taken a small, cheap room in a Paris hotel and is attempting to make herself attractive to the men she meets in cafés. Eventually a "Russian"

émigré named Nicolas Delmar is attracted to her, and he introduces her
to Serge Rubin, a Russian Jewish painter who also likes her but primar-
ily wants to sell her a painting. A young gigolo named René mistakes her for a wealthy woman
because she has an old fur coat. He stirs feelings in Sasha, but he comes
close to robbing and raping her. Some decency in him prevails, and to
her disappointment he leaves her alone. Thinking Sasha to be a prostitute, a traveling salesman in the next room in her hotel breaks in and,
mysteriously, Sasha accepts his sexual advances. Sasha may be what one
character in the text calls her, "the biggest fool I've ever met in my
life,"[2] or she may be the most compassionate and giving of women.

Good Morning, Midnight is a tough, honest, unsentimental story. A
wounded woman tells other women what it is like, having played the
roles and worn the costumes and the masks prescribed for her by society,
to find doors closing on her. Unfortunately the novel received the most
negative reception of any Rhys novel except *Quartet*. Her vision was
finally too sordid for daily and weekly reviewers (Angier, 373, 705).

Structure

Good Morning, Midnight is a first-person narrative in which Sasha relates
the events of a few days of her life, her dreams, and her memories to
form a collage of her various psychological states and her conscious and
unconscious mind. Like *Voyage in the Dark, Good Morning, Midnight* is
divided into four parts. Each part is subdivided into short, untitled,
unnumbered chapters or sections.

Part one is by far the longest. With 81 pages it is twice as long as
part four and three times the lengths of parts two and three. Again Rhys
uses the first part of a novel for a lengthy and detailed exposition, establishing time, places, characterization, themes, image patterns, and a
foreshadowing of the denouement. In part one we learn that Sasha
Jansen is newly arrived in Paris, living in a hotel room, and establishing
the routine of her life. In flashbacks Sasha informs us of her maudlin
evening in a café the night before and that she came from London,
where her friend Sidonie, sorry for Sasha because she is drinking and
getting to look old, lent her money for her trip to Paris, a city is which
she once lived and worked when she was married to Enno Jansen and
had changed her name from Sophia to Sasha.

Sasha describes the jobs she had in Paris 10 or 12 years before,
including working as a receptionist in a department store under the

aegis of an insensitive English capitalist, Mr. Blank. Other memories are of work as a shop clerk and a tourist guide for American Express.

Hating her hotel room and annoyed by a lascivious, older male guest, a *commis voyageur*, she tries to find a new, lighter room in another hotel but fails to be satisfied. Sasha's thoughts turn to a more recent sojourn in London, and she informs us that she has had a very small legacy that she accumulated to the amount 35 pounds and with which she attempted to drink herself to death.

Mountparnasse has become a microcosm of the world. In yet another café, Sasha realizes that her "life, which seems so simple and monotonous, is really a complicated affair of cafés . . . streets . . . and rooms" (*GMM*, 46). The rootless Sasha is surrounded by Dutch, Chinese, and people of other nationalities. Walking on the boulevard St. Michael, she is picked up by three Russian men, the youngest and most handsome of whom she will meet again and who will play an important part in her narrative. They are a sad group, but Sasha is glad for the company and attention. They go off drinking together, and later they take her to her hotel and make a date to meet her at four the next afternoon. Sasha is revitalized by the encounter and plans to have her graying hair dyed the next day.

The following morning, as Sasha leaves her hotel, an old beggar woman stops her, and Sasha gives her a generous sum, as if to buy off old age. Later, at lunch in a café, she grows paranoid, as she feels that everyone is looking at her. They seem to feel sorry for her, and she is moved to tears. But quickly she feels antagonistic toward a young woman in the café, but she cannot say the hard things to her she would like to utter. In a park she reminisces about a cat with an inferiority complex she once threw out of her room only to learn it had been run over by a taxi. A merciful death, she thought, almost in envy.

In Sasha's mind the date with the Russians has turned into a date with the young, handsome one. Sasha turns up for the rendezvous but cannot go in because she feels she looks terrible. Instead she returns to her room, locks her door, and dreams of the painful delivery of her child and how the midwife bandaged her like a mummy, to avoid stretch marks and save her figure.

At the hairdresser Sasha becomes a blonde. As she is planning to buy a new hat and dress, she accidentally meets the young Russian, who turns out to be Ukrainian by birth and a naturalized Frenchman named Nicolas Delmar. He offers to buy her a cup of chocolate but she wants a drink. He is respectful, sympathetic, and "comforting—almost as comforting as the hairdresser" (*GMM*, 67). Nicolas has lifted her spirits, and she even thinks she may be ready to return to London. They plan to meet at four the next day. A date and then a new hat and she is totally happy and confident.

Next Sasha is picked up by a good-looking young French Canadian, or so he says he is; in fact he is a gigolo who thinks she is a rich English woman because she has a fur coat. Sasha enjoys his line, his plea for help, his desire to be shown Paris, and his sexual attention. She plays him along and has fun, making him leave her at her hotel entrance, and she goes to bed feeling satisfied, for she has flirted and won, and she has had enough to drink. Part one ends with Sasha having provided an exposition by revealing her background and her needs and seeming to have gotten control of her life again through the attention of men and the aid of a new hair color and new clothes.

Part two continues Sasha's rejuvenation, but her heavy drinking and alcohol dependency are a danger to her. Nicolas takes her to Serge, a talented and sensitive Russian Jewish painter who is eager to sell his work but is also reluctant to part with it. On the way to the studio they pass a hotel that Sasha lived in at one of the times when she was contemplating suicide, and she remembers a long-ago encounter with a man from Lille, now faceless in her mind, who picked her up, told her many things about his life (which made her less sad), but then unceremoniously dropped her. At the studio Serge plays some "Martinique music" on an old gramophone, and Sasha recalls "lying in a hammock looking up into the branches of a tree" (*GMM*, 92). The place was between hills and the sea. Rhys seems to be signaling that her heroine has a Caribbean island background.

Both men are respectful to Sasha, even when they realize that she is not rich. They will not let her drink heavily or buy a bottle of brandy. To distract Sasha, Serge tells her about an episode in London earlier in his life when he met a mulatto woman from the Caribbean who was an alcoholic and unhappy in a relationship. He tried to comfort her and help her, but because he did not want to go to bed with her, she felt rejected and grew angry. The story seems a parallel to events in Sasha's life.

Serge leaves, perhaps so that Delmar can make love to Sasha, and when he returns Sasha generously insists on buying a painting of "an old Jew with a red nose, playing a banjo" (*GMM*, 100), a sad image that symbolizes and reflects her own marginalized state. She will pay him later that night through Nicolas. Sasha feels "exalted" by the human

contact with the sensitive painter and the admiring young man. She is
at the emotional high point of her narrative. A young man and a fine
artist have admired her and thus reassured her that she is not old or
unattractive. Her young friend is even jealous because she likes the
painter, too.

Sasha gives Nicolas the payment for the picture, not knowing if he
will pass it on to Serge, but he does. Part two ends as Sasha completes a
happy day with a meal in a bar and a visit to a cinema. Back in her room
she looks at her new picture and feels both compassion for others and
self-pity: "This damned room—it's saturated with the past. . . . It's all
the rooms I've ever slept in, all the streets I've ever walked in. Now the
whole thing moves in an ordered, undulating procession past my eyes.
Rooms, streets, streets, rooms" (GMM, 109). Clearly there are more
streets for her to walk.

Part three is one long flashback to the time just after the end of
World War I, presumably 1919 to perhaps 1921, in which Sasha
remembers meeting Enno (the man who became her husband), their
courtship, their early life together, their hand-to-mouth existence in various Continental cities, and their arrival in Paris, where just after Sasha
becomes pregnant, Enno loses interest in her and eventually leaves.
Clearly he never truly loved her, while she loved him deeply and uncon-
ditionally.

Sasha has filed her memories of that period of her life with her recollections of the rooms in which she lived, sometimes with Enno and
sometimes alone. A thought of a room and her mind fills with the
events that took place in it at that time.

Enno, who claims to have served in the French foreign legion, is supposedly a chansonnier and a journalist, and although he occasionally
gets something published, the young couple have little money, while the
money he brings in seems to come from out of the blue. Living in a
filthy room in Paris, Enno and Sasha have unsavory "friends," one of
whom hints that Enno should be pimping for Sasha (GMM, 127). Men
seem to circle the attractive girl like wolves, but she will not whore;
even a kiss that seems to be paid for nauseates her (GMM, 119–20).

Seemingly concurrent with Sasha's pregnancy, Enno loses sexual
interest in her and puts her down: " 'You don't know how to make love,'
he said. 'You're too passive, you're lazy, you bore me. I've had enough of
this' " (GMM, 128). Sasha does do some work as an English tutor, but
she is a creation of the strong Enno, and this Pygmalion is tired of his
Galatea. Sasha's son dies, "Lying so cold and still with a ticket round his

wrist" (*GMM*, 139). Sasha sums up her philosophy, "God is very cruel. . . . A devil of course" (*GMM*, 140), and Enno boards a train and rides out of Sasha's life.

The final section of part three, only 15 lines long, brings the narrative immediately to Sasha's present. She is ready to put all that trauma behind her. She understands herself: "What happened was that, as soon as I had the slightest chance of a place to hide in, I crept into it and hid. Well, sometimes it's a fine day, isn't it? Sometimes the skies are blue. Sometimes the air is light, easy to breathe. And there is always tomorrow" (*GMM*, 145). Now she has hope.

Part four is both Sasha's resurrection and *Walpurgisnacht,* her triumph and her defeat, her meeting and greeting midnight. The savior and tormentor is René, the gigolo, who unexpectedly appears at her room. She does not want to see him; nevertheless, Sasha is excited by his visit. They make a date to meet later that day, and she buys him dinner. They stop for drinks at the Deux Margot, and Sasha's thoughts flash back to the time she had a job ghostwriting fairy tales for a rich woman on the Riviera. It turns out that René knows the woman and her mansion. Sasha tells René that she is afraid, and he assumes that she is afraid that he will kill her, but she would welcome death. She confesses that she is "afraid of men . . . And I'm even more afraid of women. And I'm very much afraid of the whole bloody human race" (*GMM*, 172–73).

René and Sasha are on the way to l'Hôtel de l'Espérance. She remembers a time when a man she loved mistreated her, and then she is at the door of her hotel, where René says good night but sneaks in behind her. Realizing that he is on the dark landing beside her, she puts her arms around him and happily hugs him because René is for her "love, youth, spring, happiness, everything I thought I had lost" (*GMM*, 177). Sasha is sexually aroused, but René is insensitive and coarse, and they drink too much. She wants him to go, but he refuses, and they struggle. He almost rapes her, not out of desire but to prove his strength and exert his mastery.

Sasha manages to divert René by offering him her money; after all, he is a gigolo. Furthermore, she completely turns him off with ridicule and laughter. René leaves humiliated, but to her surprise he has not taken her money. She has won a victory: a man has been humiliated, diverted from forced sex, and has been moved not to rob her. But the victory is Pyrrhic, for at this moment she realizes that René does care a little for her, and she wishes him back. Very drunk now, she fantasies that he is returning to her, and she opens her door a little, takes off her clothes, and gets into bed. Sasha waits with her arm over her eyes, "As still as if I were dead" (*GMM*,190). However, it is not René who enters, but the despised *commis*, who has been listening to everything. Sasha realizes who is standing over her, "his mean eyes flickering" (*GMM*, 190). The last five lines of the text are among the most discussed in all of the Rhys canon: "He doesn't say anything. . . . I look straight into his eyes and despise another poor devil of a human being for the last time. . . . Then I put my arms round him and pull him down on to the bed, saying: 'Yes—yes—yes . . .' (Rhys's ellipsis) (*GMM*, 190).

Sasha's last utterance and act have been called her "Joycean affirmation" (Le Gallez,140), as if she were an imitation Molly Bloom in *Ulysses* (1922), echoing that character's final words and also saying yes to life (Kloepfer, 85–86). Coral Ann Howells says that Sasha's words are "a conscious echo of Molly Bloom's eternal female language" (Howells, 99). Helen Nebeker feels that Rhys was not only consciously alluding to Joyce but was associating Sasha's voyage with Leopold Bloom's so that Sasha, on the mythic level, is a female Ulysses (Nebeker, 117–18). Perhaps Sasha's tale is a great return from a voyage in the dark. Thomas F. Staley argues that "Sasha's last words and closing gesture are no more a grand affirmation of life than Molly Bloom's" (Staley, 98). She is a woman who in opening her body to a man she cares nothing at all for is recognizing that there is a dimension beyond the erotic in the coupling of people: the primal need for human contact. But then again, Sasha in the arms of the *commis* may be paying her masochistic penance for her sense of guilt over the past events of her life or for rejecting René and his vitality.

In this shocking scene, Sasha is not saying "yes" to life, but to death. This is not affirmation but resignation. If Rhys the modernist is making a reference to Joyce the modernist, it is as parody. The *commis* is death as traveling salesman; he goes everywhere. His sales pitch never fails. It is obscenely lascivious. He sneaks into one's room and bed, and his embrace is irresistible. Sasha, waiting naked in a bed, is not only prepared for a lover, she is ready for the grave.

The *commis*'s mystical and symbolic function is established early in the text. He is "the ghost of the landing. . . . He is as thin as a skeleton" (*GMM*, 14). He wears a "beautiful dressing-gown, immaculately white, with long, wide, hanging sleeves. . . . He looks like a priest, the priest of some obscene, half-understood religion" (*GMM*, 35).

The epigram for the text, Emily Dickinson's poem "Good morning, Midnight," provides the oxymoron for Rhys's title, and it also establishes the life versus death conflict in Sasha and her narrative, as the poem's persona says she would like to stay in the sunshine but the day is tired of her, and so "good night." Coming home to midnight is a return to oblivion.

Two geometric shapes are emblematic of the structure of this novel: the circle and the angle. Sasha has returned to Paris, but through flashbacks, her story really commences some 15 years before in the same city. She has come full circle. The angle has a long sloping leg up to the apex and then an acute descent. This figure represents Sasha's growing happiness, her new confidence in herself, and then her quick fall, like other Rhys heroines.

Following the first person, stream-of-consciousness, cinematic— quick cut, soft focus—structural pattern she established in *Quartet*, Rhys constructs in *Good Morning, Midnight* another outstanding modernist, proto-feminist novel.

Internationalism

Sasha is identified as an Englishwoman who married a foreigner and who has spent much of her life on the Continent, especially in Paris. Nevertheless, Rhys seems determined to remind her readers that she herself is neither English nor French but a person of West Indian origin who is urbanely aware of the various nationalities, cultures, and races on the globe. As part of her creative process, Rhys establishes her coterminous relationship with her heroine through encoded references to a mutual background.

Serge plays Martinique music for Sasha in his studio and dances with a black mask over his face, while Sasha day dreams of lying in a hammock with the sound of the sea in her ears (*GMM*, 92). All through the text Rhys keeps the peoples of the world moving through her scenes both in the foreground and background. The most significant male characters in the text are "exotics" and exiles. Sasha is not a common English name. She changed it from Sophia when she married Enno, perhaps having left her wisdom (Sophia) behind. She met Enno in London, but he is a Dutch man who served for a while with the French army in the early stages of World War I.

René, the gigolo, who Sasha insists is Spanish or Spanish American, claims to be French-Canadian, and he has wild tales to tell about life in Morocco and escaping from the French foreign legion. His great desire is to get to London to prey on English women. Nicolas Delmar is a Ukrainian who Sasha first assumes is a Russian. He claims to be a naturalized Frenchman who has done his military service in the French army. Serge Rubin, the sensitive artist with whom Sasha has the most empathy, is a double exile, a Jew and a Russian, who lived in London for a while, where he cared for a mulatto West Indian woman, and whose sad and lonely experience represents Rhys's identifying with a woman with black and white blood. Rhys also uses the West Indian woman to encode in the novel her own island background and her unhappy relationships as a young woman in England.

In a restaurant scene Sasha's menu lists international cuisine including Vienna steak and Welsh rabbit. Two Dutch men are talking at the next table. Five Chinese come in. The restaurant touts its "olde English atmosphere" (*GMM*, 44–45). Outside she meets the Russians whom she first takes for Germans or Scandinavians, partly because one of them looks like an actor in German films.

Rhys's relationship with Paris was a love/hate one. In Paris she had found inspiration and success as a writer, and she had been young and very beautiful. But Paris is where her marriage failed, where she lost her first child, where she had experienced great poverty and loneliness, and where a mentor-lover had betrayed her. The great city was world enough for her. Delmar speaks for all when he says, "Have you ever noticed . . . that when you go from one part of Paris to another, it's like going from one town to another—even from one country to another? The people are different, the atmosphere is different, even the women dress differently" (*GMM*, 66).

Serge, the Russian Jew, makes "authentic" West African masks (*GMM*, 91). He serves porto wine in Japanese saké cups (*GMM*, 93). Sasha is informed that the best place in Paris to hear "negro music" is at the Cuban Cabin in Montmartre (*GMM*, 91). Serge's London experience centers on his platonic relationship with the "Martiniquaise" (*GMM*, 95–98). Enno's friend Alfred, who hints that Enno should pimp for Sasha, is a Turk. A Russian whom Sasha tutors loves Oscar Wilde's work. A Hindu bookshop assistant sells her a "very good book, very beautiful, most true" (*GMM*, 132). It's about the white-slave traffic. A meal in an Algerian restaurant makes Sasha ill (*GMM*, 132). It is a small world, but Paris is a large enough world by itself. Rhys makes it a microcosm. Not only does the great city have samples of all the world's races and nationalities, it also has all the world's problems because it, too, is the sum of its people.

Themes

Alienation

Alienation is the major theme of *Good Morning, Midnight*. Sasha does not belong anywhere. She sees the question in people's eyes everywhere: "What is she doing here, the stranger, the alien, the old one?" (*GMM*, 54). And Sasha does not contest the collective judgment she encounters: "I quite agree too" (GMM, 54). The continual lack of acceptance has caused her "all the time" to ask herself, "what the devil am I doing here?" (GMM, 54). Perhaps Sasha does not know what she is doing in life, in the world of the young, in the world of the living. She hears herself being called the old woman: "la Vielle." She is totally marginalized in Paris until some men give her a temporary identity through their desire either for her money or her body. In the end, isolated, rejected, alone, she becomes, with the unnamed *commis*, only a body, and Rhys ironically has her accept that dehumanization as if it were fair, just, correct, and her due.

Rhys was almost totally marginalized by the male dominated 1930s British literary establishment, and thus the theme of alienation may be the way she surfaced her repressed anger for being wrongly ignored.

Alcohol Abuse

The Rhys heroine continues her alcohol abuse and dependency. Sasha seems always in need of a drink, sometimes desperately so. Although she is enjoying the attention of her two "Russians" in Serge's studio, she needs alcohol and becomes angry when deprived of it: "I have an irresistible longing for a long, strong drink to make me forget. . . . I say in a loud, aggressive voice: 'Go out and get a bottle of brandy,' take money out of my purse and offer it to him" (*GMM*, 94). When previously offered a tiny cup of wine, she thinks with indignation, "That, a drink!" (*GMM*, 94).

Sasha's need to control her own life takes a wrong and sorry turn when she substitutes controlling her source of alcohol for more significant manifestations of independence. She says of Delmar, "I can't stand this business of not being able to have what I want to drink, because he won't allow me to pay and certainly doesn't want to pay himself. It's too wearing" (*GMM*, 103).

On an evening out alone Sasha drinks Pernod after Pernod, before and after the cinema, and then thinks, "If I have a bottle of Bordeaux at

dinner I'll be as drunk as I'd hoped to be" (*GMM*, 109). Out of habit
and addiction, at this stage in her narrative Sasha is drinking more and
more, seeking a nighttime oblivion through alcohol and luminal even
though she is happier and more understanding of herself than she has
been since the early days of her marriage.

Sasha's night of fall and crash with René and the *commis* is lubricated
with glasses of Pernod, brandy, and bottles of wine. Her libido is first
drowned, then resuscitated and inflamed by the thought but not the
reality of René's body. Finally, with intellect turned off and thought
blotted out, she opens her arms to the despised *commis*.

There is no denial. Rhys does not flinch in her portrayal of a woman's
abuse of alcohol, implicitly condemning the addiction yet also understanding the need for the release that drugs provide from the pain of an
untenable reality.

Women against Women

In *Good Morning, Midnight* Rhys continues to reinforce her heroines'
alienation and isolation because of their, and presumably her, distrust of
other women. The Rhys heroine is misanthropic. Women are half of
humankind and thus dangerous, if not as destructive as men. Looking
out of the window of her room, Sasha observes a girl at an open window
making up. They see each other, and the girl "averts her eyes, her
expression hardens." Sasha continues, "I realize that if I watch her mak-
ing-up she will retaliate at me when I do the same thing" (*GMM*, 34).
Sasha shuts her window and moves away from it. The other women in
Rhys's earlier novels are always hostile, and the protagonists are either
hostile in return or they repress anger or flee in tears.

When Serge tells Sasha about his experience with the woman from
Martinique, he informs her that among the woman's tormentors was a
little girl who told her that "she was a dirty woman, that she smelt bad"
(*GMM*, 97). The child continues: "I hate you and I wish you were dead"
(*GMM*, 97). The girl hates a woman she hardly knows. Why? Because
she is a stranger who looks different, or because this is how females feel
toward each other from behavior inculcated from childhood? "Only
seven or eight, yet she knew so exactly how to be cruel and who it was
safe to be cruel to" (*GMM*, 98). The vignette of the child and the
woman from Martinique reminds one of the cruel children in Richard
Hughes's Caribbean novel, *A High Wind in Jamaica* (1929), which Rhys
had read (O'Connor, 221).

In a bar a woman gives Sasha "one of those looks: What do you want here, you?" (*GMM*, 104). The near paranoid Sasha thinks that another woman "is going to giggle or say something about me in a voice loud enough for me to hear" (*GMM*, 104). But Sasha has no mercy herself for other women. She sees a young woman slaving as a dishwasher, but instead of feeling sympathy, she says, "Sorry for her? Why should I be sorry for her? Hasn't she got sturdy legs and curly hair?" (*GMM*, 105). As if good looks compensate for economic exploitation.

Sasha sums up Rhys's attitude toward her sex at the time she was writing *Good Morning, Midnight* with these words: "God, it's funny, being a woman!" (*GMM*, 104). Yet Sasha remembers once having seen a girl in a bordello whom she could have loved. René asks Sasha if the prostitute ever made love to her, and she denies it almost too vigorously, but she "wanted to put my arms round her, kiss her eyes and comfort her—and if that's not love, what is?" (*GMM*, 161). But seeing a girl in a bordello and wanting to hold her is not love. René is talking about the sex act, and Sasha is in a bordello. Why? Working, buying, visiting with a male friend? Sasha seems to echo the contemporary heterosexual male evaluation of women as sexual objects to slake lust and otherwise to be disdained.

Characterization

Sasha so completely dominates the text that Enno, René, Nicolas, and Serge are mere satellites circling a moon. Basically, *Good Morning, Midnight* is the journey of a woman trying to return to a period of her life when she was deeply in love, when, early in her marriage, she still believed in men, and before the collapsing events of her life: the death of her child, desertion by her husband, job failure, alcoholism, and aimless drifting.

Rhys developed Sasha's character as if she were writing a play. After introducing her in the present, flashbacks and dreams offer chronological and psychological exposition. Returning to the present, Sasha's narrative moves through the rising action of her growing happiness and sense of control of her life to the dramatic climax of her struggle for mastery with René and the quick and shocking falling action to the catastrophe of the *commis*'s obscene embrace. This dramatic quality motivated Selma vaz Dias to script the story for the British Broadcasting Corporation radio play that led to the rediscovery of Jean Rhys.

Sasha, like Hamlet, tries to write her own play and create a role for herself that she can finally live with and comfortably project. But as with Hamlet her act is too good. It proves dangerous when she convinces René that she is a deep and serious woman of the world in control of her life and not interested in an emotional or sexual relationship with him. She has a need to get back at men: "This is where I might be able to get some of my own back. You talk to them, you pretend to sympathize; then, just at the last moment when they are not expecting it, you say: 'Go to Hell' " (*GMM*, 72). But she takes her revenge on men on the wrong man, one who cares and whom she really desires.

Sasha is more mature than Rhys's previous heroines, and we like her somewhat better, perhaps because she *is* more mature and therefore does not place the blame for her misfortunes on other people. She knows her paranoia and contradictions, although she cannot overcome their effects.[3] Sasha's idea of happiness is often expressed in her opportunities to make herself attractive to men, such as at the hairdressers' or especially shopping, which is an aesthetic experience, indeed almost a sexual experience for her. At the very high point of her narrative, at the end of part three, when she is happy and hopeful, she decides "Tomorrow I'll go to the Galeries Lafayette, choose a dress, . . . buy gloves, buy scent, buy lipstick . . . Just the sensation of spending, that's the point. I'll look at bracelets studded with artificial jewels, red, green and blue, necklaces of imitation pearls, cigarette-cases, jeweled tortoises. . . . And when I have had a couple of drinks I shan't know whether it's yesterday, today or tomorrow" (*GMM*, 145).

The dessert of a happy experience, of course, is alcohol. The ultimate happiness is satiety and oblivion. Rhys is depicting a compulsive consumerism embraced by women who must compete with other women through painting their faces and decorating their bodies to attract or keep the sexual interest of men. In other words, to consume is to consummate.

Enno is a heartless, selfish man, a poor provider as husband and father-to-be. He never loves Sasha. She is a beautiful possession for him, and he soon tires of her. He comes and goes without explanation. He has little success as a songwriter and a journalist, and somehow he is connected to shady individuals. Enno's character and his relationship with Sasha are blurred for us because they are filtered and dimmed through her memory, time, her bitterness, and the result of too many years of heavy drinking and using sleeping pills.

Nicolas Delmar is a young man who "lives by a code" (Nebeker, 101) in which he tries to be a gentleman who, for example, will not allow a woman to pay for anything even if she prefers to and even if it means she must do without what she wants because he is poor. He treats Sasha with genuine respect and helps her to rebuild her ego. Sasha's life would be better if she could embrace his fatalistic philosophy, "You didn't ask to be born, you didn't make the world as it is, you didn't make yourself as you are. Why torment yourself? Why not take life as it comes? You have the right to; you are not one of the guilty ones" (*GMM*, 64). Alas, he has no sex appeal for Sasha, partly because he has no economic power, and she can embrace neither his body nor his pragmatism.

The Russian Jewish painter Serge represents the best qualities of the artist: respect for his work, generosity, compassion, concern for other humans. Like other artists he is temperamental and sometimes unreliable. He offers Sasha the possibility of an intellectual, platonic friendship, but this is not what she thinks she needs. Her associations with men must always be a struggle for emotional domination and economic control. Friendship plays no significant part in the relationship between Sasha and men.

René is the most interesting, well-developed, and complex of the male characters in *Good Morning, Midnight*. He is young, handsome, sensitive, charming, everything that attracts Sasha and therefore, because he is a man, the more dangerous. Yet even though René first wanted to use this "rich" older woman to obtain a passport to London, he is the first man we meet who is genuinely interested in hearing Sasha's narrative, thus acknowledging her humanity. "He is Sasha's dream figure, almost as much as the *commis* is her nightmare" (Angier, 398). René represents Sasha's lost opportunity, a last chance that she perversely destroys by cruelly punishing him for being just what she knows he is. René takes his humiliation and leaves. He accepts the events of the evening as a comedy, and paradoxically the events become part of Sasha's tragedy.

Narrative Technique

The essence of the narrative technique in *Good Morning, Midnight* is the dramatic use of the unities of action and time. A single plot, the fall of Sasha Jansen, and a fusion of years through flashbacks and dreams into a very few days, almost creating the impression that the action occurs in a single day, from her awakening in her room at the beginning of the text to the midnight when she embraces the old *commis*.

The novel is as lean and pared away as possible. Rhys values and practices literary economy. The text "feels" as if it has been rewritten and sharpened several times so that it is as slim as one of Rhys's mannequins. Sometimes the text seems almost too refined, as with the descriptions of the character and actions of Enno, which remain somewhat blurred.

Rhys uses a system of thought dialogue when Sasha, prevented from saying or doing what she really wants to do by the mores of the patriarchal society in which she exists, represses her anger, and in a silent, frustrated woman's monologue tells herself and us what she would like to say. For example, when the odious English capitalist, Mr. Blank, is easing Sasha out of her job, she thinks, "Well, let's argue this out, Mr. Blank" (*GMM*, 29), and then silently tears into him. But she is an intimidated woman in front of a man who has called her an imbecile and who has all the power in the relationship. Thus, sadly, this woman merely demonstrates her rightful anger to herself and the reader. She curses Blank in her heart, but as it is not heard by him it can have no effect.

Imagery

In *Good Morning, Midnight* Rhys continues her use of architectonic image patterns established in earlier texts. Significant iterative images, serving the same functions as in *After Leaving Mr. Mackenzie* and *Voyage in the Dark,* are those of animals, masks, and the water drowning. But by far the most significant thematic image in *Good Morning, Midnight* is that of the room, the prison cell of the Rhys heroine's life sentence.

The text opens in Sasha's hotel room, which has "the smell of cheap hotels" (*GMM*, 9). The room talks to Sasha: " 'Quite like old times,' the room says. 'Yes? No?' " The answer of course is yes. The woman has lived most of her adult life in the "room." When Sasha wishes to move, to leave the ominous hotel and the landing she shares with the *commis*, hoping to find a "beautiful room" in another hotel, she fails, and the *commis* is waiting for her on the landing, blocking her way in his flannel nightshirt (*GMM*, 34). The new room would have been her salvation. She thinks, "I shall exist on a different plane at once if I can get this room. . . . It will be an omen. Who says you can't escape your fate? I'll escape from mine, into room 219. Just try me, just give me a chance" (*GMM*, 37).

But Sasha does not take the new room, and so her first room in the text is her destined last room. She cannot escape it any more than she can escape the grave. The final room welcomes her back: "You didn't go off then," the room comments. Sasha replies, "No, no I thought better of it. Here I belong and here I'll stay" (*GMM*, 39).

Conclusion

Jean Rhys intuitively understood that significant art must be simultaneously immediate and resistant, accessible as well as profound. In *Good Morning, Midnight*, with great skill Rhys has portrayed a terrible life in transit, dragging along all of its psychological baggage. She has told the saga of a defeated woman with irony, vicious satire, and even some sardonic humor. *Good Morning, Midnight* is never sentimental. Sasha's world is one in which the struggle for dominance between women and men is programmed by economic power and ruined by the inevitable use of that power.

Unlike in the earlier novels, the heroine of *Good Morning, Midnight* has a little money, a small stake from a female friend, but her money hardly liberates her. Rather, it seems to have cut her off from the community of women, and it prevents a relationship with poorer men except when the usual transactional hierarchy is overturned and the woman is the buyer. And even then money offered but not taken ruins the relationship.

The lost and crippled Jean Rhys heroine, from her West Indian childhood, seduction and abandonment in London, misuse by the Heidlers, betrayal by a husband, and abuse by other Englishmen in Paris, to her penance, sacrifice, and degradation at the end of *Good Morning, Midnight*, is one of the great creations of modernist literature. Rhys is as unsparing of that heroine as Zola is of Nana, and it is not a coincidence that the "tart" book Anna is reading early in *Voyage in the Dark* is *Nana* (*V*, 9–10).

In their stripped, unsentimental depiction of urban life, the four novels seem almost more French than English. Each is successively finer yet more painful to read because the reader soon realizes that not only has an individual woman been lost, but a potentially useful life has been wasted by a society that does not value or understand a woman's mind, sensitive nature, and compassionate heart. With the publication of *Good Morning, Midnight*, Jean Rhys entered the nighttime of her career. She would not be published again until the 1960s.

Chapter Seven
Wide Sargasso Sea

In 1966 Jean Rhys crossed her gulf of silence to *Wide Sargasso Sea*. The novel is indisputably her masterpiece. If the earlier four novels are exercises in revenge on the men in Rhys's life who hurt or betrayed her, most of whom were English, *Wide Sargasso Sea* is Rhys's revenge on all Englishmen. This retribution is personified in the character of Edward Rochester (the family name never appears in Rhys's text), Charlotte Brontë's tarnished hero in *Jane Eyre* (1847) and Jean Rhys's hero-villain, her finest and most profound male portrayal. The itinerant Rhys heroine in the body of Antoinette Cosway (renamed Bertha Mason by her insufferable husband) is now driven to madness, "the madwoman in the attic,"[1] and to her self-immolation at Thornfield Hall.

Rhys may have chosen the title for her one novel set almost entirely in the West Indies from Ezra Pound's poem "Portrait of a Lady" (1916), which Ford Madox Ford conceivably could have shown her in Paris in the early 1920s, when Pound was Ford's friend. The poem is about the gifts an intelligent woman can offer, and the first line is, "Your mind and you are our Sargasso Sea."

The Sargasso Sea, in the North Atlantic, lies between the Azores and the West Indies, dividing and uniting Europe and the Caribbean. It also stands, in Rhys's novel, "between whites and blacks, the colonizers and colonized . . . the possessors and the possessed" (O'Connor, 145). Furthermore it stands for the murky entrapping place of the libido dividing and uniting women and men.

Wide Sargasso Sea evolves out of and is different from Rhys's earlier novels in that it combines their expressionism with powerful mythic symbolism[2] in the manner of James Joyce, Virginia Woolf, and to a lesser extent D. H. Lawrence, for Rhys's last novel is about good and evil, a mysterious journey from a small island of birth and freedom to a large island of imprisonment and death, the woman's nightmare of capture and bondage, and the archetypal male struggle to master female sexuality.

Wide Sargasso Sea is a prequel to *Jane Eyre*, which Rhys read in 1939 and then conceived the idea for the novel that would prove to be her last. But *Wide Sargasso Sea* is different from most other prequels and sequels to earlier classics in that it is a repudiation of its predecessor, indicting Edward Rochester and exposing a character totally undeserving of Brontë's compassion, Miss Eyre's acceptance, and his ultimately happy fate in the Victorian masterpiece. *Jane Eyre* is romantic, full of Gothic passion, and significant in that it presents, almost for the first time, an intelligent, self-respecting Victorian woman of very modest means who takes control of her life and who makes her own way in the world. It was completely natural for Rhys to relate to and focus on the "Other" woman, the West Indian import, whom she saw as the victim of English patriarchal oppression and of the horror of women's sexuality in Brontë's novel. Rhys's revenge is not merely on those controlling, duplicitous, women-hating Englishmen and on the cold nation she never accepted as her own but, shrewdly, on the sacred canon of British literature; thus the brilliant subversion of *Jane Eyre*. Major reviewers were ecstatic, calling the novel "a magnificent comeback," "astonishingly convincing," and "a rare synthesis of the baroque and the precise" (Angier, 578, 724).

   Wide Sargasso Sea is set just after the freeing of the slaves in the British colonies under the Emancipation Act of 1 August 1838. Destined for a horrible death (that has already happened to her in *Jane Eyre*), Antoinette Cosway is a Jamaican heiress who partly tells her story out of her madness while locked in an attic room at Thornfield Hall in England by her husband Edward, with an attendant, Grace Poole. Antoinette's story is also added to by Edward and Grace. Antoinette is the daughter of Annette Cosway Mason, who was the beautiful younger second wife of the deceased planter Alexander Cosway. Antoinette was about 10 when her dissolute father died, and for five frightening years she, her mother Annette, and her imbecile brother Pierre remained on the family plantation, Coulibri, living in poverty and with only the company of a few former slaves. Eager for security the impoverished young widow marries Mr. Mason, an affable, generous, but foolish Englishman who has come to Jamaica to make a killing during the economic shambles that followed the emancipation.

   Mason introduces English customs and ways, brings in English friends, and allows Annette to restore the mansion and the plantation. He is obtuse to the dangers presented by the freed Blacks, who harbor deep grievances and resentments against the "white cockroaches" who are still their economic oppressors if no longer their masters and mistresses. Annette, who has lived with the Blacks all her life, justly fears their pent-up rage but cannot convince her foolhardy, imperialist husband of the danger. One night the ex-slaves riot and burn the Masons out. Poor Pierre dies of burns. Antoinette is stoned by her Black girlfriend and childhood companion, someone she identified with. Annette's worst nightmare has come true. In the conflagration engulfing the great house, her beloved parrot is burned alive, and she goes mad. Antoinette requires six weeks to recover from the trauma and never is able to recall all the events of the terrible night. She learns of her brother's death and sees that her mad mother has become the sexual slave of the Blacks attending her.

Mr. Mason genuinely cares for his stepdaughter, and he sends her to a convent school to be educated. Upon his death she receives a legacy of £30,000. She is now of marriageable age, and her stepbrother Richard Mason arranges a match for her with Edward Rochester, a younger son without a fortune who must marry rich or remain poor. He goes to Jamaica for Antoinette, who is now a beautiful woman of about 18 and who at first does not want the pale, sea sickish, and unacclimatized Englishman but finally accepts him as her husband. They journey to the Windward Islands to honeymoon on an estate that Annette once possessed. There Edward meets Christophine, Antoinette's old Black nurse and confidant, who is also an Obeah (voodoo) woman. Initially Edward is taken with the exoticness of the place and the glorious sexuality of his wife. But after a short while he tires of both and feels that his life is indolent and debilitating. To make matters worse, he receives a letter from one Daniel Cosway, who claims to be an illegitimate half brother to Antoinette. Daniel states that Annette is a mad nymphomaniac, that Antoinette has Black blood in her, and that she had sexual relations before Edward, who is infuriated, as expected from a Victorian male who assumes his property was concealed damaged goods when contracted for.

Calling her Bertha instead of the "decadent" French Antoinette, he takes her out of her lascivious environment to England to imprison her and to control and punish her sexuality. Finally, insane now because of her ill treatment, "Bertha" waits in her bed for the moment when her keeper, Grace Poole, will fall asleep so she can escape the prison room and light the symbolic and real fire that will blind her husband, destroy his home, and take her life.

Structure

Structurally, *Wide Sargasso Sea* is the most audacious of Rhys's novels. The text is divided into three parts, each subdivided into short, untitled sections. Antoinette speaks the first part, about a third of the book. Edward narrates nearly all of the second part, almost two-thirds of the novel, with the exception of an 11-page section in which Antoinette tells of her visit to Christophine for aid and comfort. In the third part, only 14 pages, Grace Poole describes how Antoinette came into her charge, and Antoinette continues her narrative.

Part one establishes "the psycho-historical background for Antoinette's life" (Staley, 102). We learn of the experiences and traumas of her childhood that formed her consciousness, fixated her in childlike dependence and passivity, and doomed her relationship with an English-man from across the Sargasso Sea. She has grown up in an atmosphere of smoldering hatred and recrimination, alternation between poverty and affluence, cultural conflicts and misunderstandings, and the social and economic consequences of the emancipation.

Antoinette remembers her lush and exotic family estate in its heyday and introduces Christophine, her Black nurse, who, like Antoinette's mother, came from Martinique. Antoinette is a bridesmaid at her mother's wedding to Mr. Mason, and she learns that her father was a womanizer.[3] Antoinette sees an Obeah animal sacrifice and is frightened by the slaughter and blood, a foreboding of the bloodshed to come (WSS, 31). Annette wants to leave Coulibri, but Mr. Mason is foolishly unafraid.

Antoinette does not grow close to her kind stepfather, but she realizes that he has saved her family. To his amusement she calls him her "white pappy" (WSS, 33). One night the Blacks riot and set fire to the house. Annette screams at Mason, "I told you what would happen again and again. . . . You would not listen, you sneered at me, you grinning hypocrite, you ought not to live either, you know so much, don't you? Why don't you go out and ask them to let you go? Say how innocent you are. Say you have always trusted them" (WSS, 40).

The power structure has been temporarily reversed. Outside the burning mansion a Black yells, "But look the black Englishman! Look the white niggers!" (WSS, 42) and the Blacks begin to stone the family group. Mason prays for a miracle and it comes. Annette's parrot, Coco, is seen on the upper railings of the house. He is on fire, and he tries to fly away but falls in flames. It is unlucky to kill a parrot, so the Blacks draw aside and let the family proceed to their carriage to make their escape. Antoinette runs for comfort to her friend Tia, who throws a stone at her. The girls are torn between love and hate: "We stared at each other, blood on my face, tears on hers. It was as if I saw myself. Like in a looking glass" (WSS, 45).

Still, Antoinette's identification with Christophine's people is lost. The disaster at Coulibri is the most traumatic event of Antoinette's childhood. It takes her six weeks to recover from the shock, and when she is herself again she learns that her brother Pierre is dead and her mother has been sent to the country to live. Antoinette insists upon visiting Annette with Christophine and there realizes that her mother is not the rational woman she had been before the attack on the house. Furthermore, her mother is under the sexual domination of a Black man, and this fact becomes a part of the deep current of Black-White sexuality in the text.

Mason places Antoinette in a convent school, where other students mistreat her. A mulatto boy named Sandi Cosway comes to her rescue. He is a cousin, one of many mixed-blood relatives that the male Cosways have engendered on the island. The nuns are kind and supportive, and Antoinette loves some of them, but she has a recurring bad dream in the convent school of walking away for Coulibri with a man who will sexually assault her and perhaps kill her (*WSS*, 60). Antoinette reveals, "I dreamed I was in Hell" (*WSS*, 60). The convent is her refuge from the predatory world outside, but she is not destined to live her life within its secure walls. The psychologically scarred girl must soon begin to endure her life in the schizophrenic world her destiny has prepared for her, suspended between two cultures and two races. Each will identify her with the other, and she will find acceptance nowhere.

Part two is Edward's account: his success in making a financially advantageous match, his failure to overcome his Byronic pride, his sexual repression, his Victorian values, his racial prejudice, and his inability to accept his wife for the woman she is, a natural, passionate, and loyal person. It begins with his and Antoinette's arrival on an island in the Windward Islands on their way to their honeymoon place, Granbois, her mother's old estate. It is raining, foreshadowing the trouble and the tears to come. Edward proudly and prejudiciously refuses to take shelter in a Black woman's hut, thus introducing the theme of racial bigotry in the text. He relates the very favorable (to him) facts of the wedding settlement: £30,000 without conditions and, fatally for Antoinette, no provisions for settlement for her in case of separation or divorce. She has no rights under English law to any of the money or property left her by her stepfather.

Edward meets Christophine at the estate and is suspicious and jealous of her from the beginning. He writes a letter to his father, thus providing more exposition. It relates that Mr. Mason conveniently died shortly after Edward sailed for the West Indies, and Antoinette's stepbrother Richard negotiated the marriage agreement. Edward became ill for several weeks almost upon arrival in Jamaica. Later he recalls what he can of the wedding ceremony, particularly remembering that he thought friends of the family were inexplicably showing pity for him: "But why should they pity me. I who have done so well for myself?" (*WSS*, 77). Despite a fortune of a dowry and a beautiful young bride (his order of preference), Edward is unsure of the bargain and is beginning to feel that there were unspoken handicaps accompanying Antoinette.

Edward's thoughts go back to before the wedding, and the reader learns that Antoinette at first refused him, to the great chagrin and anger of Richard Mason. Antoinette would not give her reason, and so the desperate suitor goes to her to implore her to trust him, promising that he will provide happiness and that elusive state Rhys's heroines are always vainly seeking: "peace." Prophetically, Antoinette is "afraid of what may happen" (*WSS*, 78–79). Passively, to avoid hurting Edward, Antoinette consents without a word and with only a nod.

At first the newlyweds are happy in their hill country retreat. But a letter to Edward from the supposed half brother Daniel Cosway sows seeds of doubt as to the wisdom of his marriage choice and distrust of the veracity and virtue of his bride. Has she had sex before him? is her mother mad? is she alive or dead? will Antoinette go mad also? The novel takes on a Gothic atmosphere when, overwhelmed by the luxuriant island and the strangeness of the inhabitants, Edward begins to study Obeah: "I have noticed that Negroes as a rule refuse to discuss the black magic in which so many believe. Voodoo as it is called in Haiti— Obeah in some of the islands" (*WSS*, 107). His interest in Obeah, or Voodoo, implies a connection to his later treatment of Antoinette, what may be described as a symbolic zombification.[4]

The couple are no longer happy or compatible as the doubt eats at Edward. Antoinette journeys to where Christophine is now living to get a love potion, while Edward is visiting the despicable Daniel, where his doubts are further and fully inflamed to the point that he is sure his wife is deceitful and has had sexual relations with others, especially her cousin Sandi. Knowing for sure that Antoinette's mother went mad, he is willing to believe that Antoinette is mad, too.

Returning to Granbois, Edward refuses first to listen to and then to accept and believe Antoinette's explanations of the traumatic events in her earlier life. Although they no longer have been sleeping together, a dose of Christophine's love potion, secretly placed in his wine, enflames

Edward with lust, but after making love with his wife he seeks out the beautiful but conniving Black servant Amélie and has sex with her in a room separated from Antoinette's bedroom by only a door. He does this vicious act for revenge on Antoinette for all her supposed transgressions, which of course exist only in his self-tortured brain. Later we learn that Antoinette heard everything.

Antoinette and Edward begin to drink heavily, she more than he. Drunk, she grows violent and irrational in her unhappiness and disappointment, while Edward has come in a short time to hate his wife. Christophine intervenes to try to help Antoinette, asking Edward to give his wife a part of the money she received as her dowry so she can leave him, but he refuses. She then asks if he will take Antoinette back to his bed and give her love again, but he refuses that, too. Christophine can do no more.

Edward plans to take Antoinette back to Jamaica and on to England to punish and imprison her. "She'll not laugh in the sun again. She'll not dress up and smile at herself in that damnable looking glass. . . . Vain, silly creature. Made for loving? Yes, but she'll have no lover, for I don't want her and she'll see no other. . . . She said she loved this place. This is the last she'll see of it" (WSS, 165). They depart Granbois.

Part three depicts Antoinette's/Bertha's fate and there couples with Jane Eyre. In it Rhys overcomes "the anxiety of influence" by demolishing a given in the great predecessor, that mad, dumb, murdering Bertha was merely a cross to bear for the suffering Edward Rochester, so that no reader who knows Wide Sargasso Sea will ever see Jane Eyre in the same light again.

First Grace Poole informs us how she came to be employed by Edward to guard and tend his mad Jamaican wife and that she has remained in the unpleasant job because of its security. Her charge is always dangerous: "I'll say one thing for her, she hasn't lost her spirit. She's still fierce. I don't turn my back on her when her eyes have that look" (WSS, 178).

Then Antoinette resumes her narrative, relating how she watches Poole and steals some of the gin when Grace has drunk herself to sleep. She recalls being violent on a ship, but does not now know where she is. Her stepbrother has come to visit her, but she barely remembers it. She recalls her romance with Sandi, the last happy period in her life. One night she dreams of stealing the keys to the room, escaping into the house, setting fire to it, climbing to the battlements of the mansion, and jumping back to her happy childhood at Coulibri. She awakes and proceeds to make reality of her dream. Thus through Rhys a great colonial secret, the truth of Bertha, is let out (Howells, 108).

A Post-Colonial Caribbean Text

Jean Rhys probably never thought of her final novel as a major contribution to post-colonial Caribbean literature, but many significant aspects of the text are charged with an acute awareness of imperial/colonial, Black/White, and planter/worker antagonisms and conflicts that are compounded with mutual dependence.

The Black/White conflict is foregrounded. The child Antoinette has a fond playmate in Tia, but when the races are facing off, friendship falls victim to hatred. It is not a lesson that a child forgets. Struck in the head by Tia's stone, Antoinette later learns that the wound on her forehead will not leave a physical scar, but the emotional scar is for life.

On the other hand Christophine is Antoinette's surrogate mother, good friend, advisor, and would-be savior first of Annette and later Antoinette. Because of Christophine, Antoinette never hates Blacks but respects and even envies Black society and culture. She has never been totally imbued with White creole racism even though it is all around her. She holds no racial grudge that she and her family were burned out of Coulibri and that her mad mother was sexually exploited by a Black man. When she is angry with servants, as she is with Amélie, who has made herself sexually available to Edward, there is no racial taint to her anger, and she is quickly forgiving as one woman to another. It is Christophine who punishes Amélie. Edward is the one who has trouble with color, not only of skin but of the bright greens and purples and blues of the Caribbean world. Antoinette's essential innocence and lack of sophistication are part of her island heritage. She does not know the conniving, treacherous ways of Europe. It is a fatal flaw.

Edward's discomfit with the light of the Caribbean and his cold nature symbolize the clash of England and the Caribbean Islands. At the end of the text, when Antoinette/Bertha sets out to burn down Thornfield Hall, the fire of retribution ignited by the angry Blacks at Coulibri comes around to destroy the exploiter's home mansion, too. Thus, "*Wide Sargasso Sea* directly contests British sovereignty—of persons, of place, of culture, of language. It reinvests its own hybridized world with an authoritative perspective, but one that is deliberately constructed as provisional since the novel is at pains to demonstrate the subjective nature of a point of view and hence the cultural construction of 'meaning' " (Tiffin, 23).

Themes

Female/Male Relations

The great theme of *Wide Sargasso Sea* is the nature of the heterosexual relationship: the great gulf that divides men and women, the rocks and shoals endangering the voyage together, the apparent truth that men and women always come from different cultures, and that male culture dominates even on the female's home ground. One aspect of the conflict within the heterosexual couple, Rhys implies, is that the man, like Edward, never fully commits, always holds back something, maintains an ambivalence in the relationship as if to commit fully were to give up manly control, to be Samson within the power of a Delilah. He is always suspicious that the woman does not, cannot love him, and love him exclusively.

A woman like Antoinette, forever innocent and yet so in touch with her basic sexuality, a being of the sun, the sky, the tropical forest and the rain, warm, open, and generous, loves wholeheartedly and without conditions, and that is the source of her vulnerability.

It is Christophine, the nurse-protector of Antoinette (like St. Christopher, who cared for and carried the Christ child), who understands the truth of heterosexual relationships, that few men will help the women they supposedly love when those women are troubled. She says of Edward, "This is not a man who will help you when he sees you break up. Only the best can do that. The best—and sometimes the worst" (*WSS*, 156). She advises the distraught Antoinette to pretend that she is ill, to tell Edward that she wishes to visit a cousin in Martinique, to ask Edward for some money for the trip, and to stay away and take care of herself—then Edward would desire her back. But, out of love and simple integrity, Antoinette cannot take that course. Emotionally committed to her husband and socially programmed to stay in a marriage regardless of consequence, she opts for a love potion to magically renew Edward's desire for her.

For Rhys neither love nor sex is the binding factor in female/male relationships, especially marriage; power is. Antoinette is doomed to powerlessness, and thus loss of her husband's respect, through the social conditioning she has endured as well as British law and the constraints of Victorian patriarchy. *Wide Sargasso Sea* depicts a colonial society in chaos, being taken over by nouveau riche and reorganizing in the process of going from a slave to a free society. Yet although Blacks are emancipated, women like Antoinette remain in slavery, as chattels to their husbands, and they are more passive than the slaves were in their bondage. As the ex-slaves revenge the past by burning Coulibri, so Antoinette emancipates herself and takes revenge by burning Thornfield Hall.

Culture, Class, Color in Conflict

From her earliest remembered experiences, Antoinette was aware of racial differences and involved in racial tension. Indeed, Thorunn Lonsdale points out that "all of Jean Rhys's depictions of childhood are based in the West Indies and are centered on white creole children, and there is clear awareness of racial difference. The difference tends to be described with ambivalence or hostility. Yet, paradoxically, the nurturing female children receive is predominantly from black servants."[5]

The result for children like Antoinette is confused cultural identity and a resulting diminishing sense of self. They take refuge in received societal responses. When the child Antoinette is angered by Christophine's teasing her over three pennies, she bursts out with "keep them then, you cheating nigger" (*WSS*, 24). Christophine, who loyally remains with Antoinette's family and brings them through hard times, really does not think that the girl and her mother are true Whites because she sees "whiteness" in economic or class terms: "Real white people, they got gold money. They didn't look at us. . . . Old time white people nothing but white nigger now, and black nigger better than white nigger" (*WSS*, 24).

Antoinette's mother, Annette, owes her survival to loyal Black servants, yet when Antoinette appears in her Black friend Tia's dress, she says, "Throw away that thing. Burn it" (*WSS*, 25). Her white child must not be seen in or "contaminated" by a dress once worn by a Black child, and the offending garment must be destroyed. Despite her good personal relations with Blacks, the remarried Annette wishes to leave Coulibri because she is aware of the hatred of the Black people there (*WSS*, 32). In her fear is respect. Her husband says, "Didn't you fly at me like a little wild cat when I said nigger" (*WSS*, 32). The fatuous Mr. Mason sees the Blacks as harmless: "They're too damn lazy to be dangerous" (*WSS*, 32). His lack of understanding of his neighbors nearly costs him his life.

Culture and color clashes distort life in colonial society. Daniel
Cosway is despised by Edward, Antoinette, and indeed by Rhys, but a
reader with a little emotional distance from the time and place of the
text can appreciate how his position as neither Black nor White, admiring the White lifestyle without the money to sustain it and denied by
the man he believed to be his father, could warp him and lead him to
make as much mischief as he does.

Rhys has no answer to the problems of race, class, and culture for her
time or ours. It is significant that she felt them, understood them
overtly and subconsciously, and portrayed them. As to the fate of Black
people in the Caribbean after "emancipation," it is wise Christophine
who speaks Rhys's knowledge: "No more slavery! She had to laugh!
'These new ones have Letter of the Law. Same thing. They got magistrate. They got fine. They got jail house and chain gang. They got tread
machine to mash up people's feet. New ones worse than old ones—more
cunning, that's all' " (WSS, 26). This passage may be Rhys's apologia for
the old slave-holding West Indian class with which she may have
romantically identified (Lonsdale, 64), but the words here are without
authorial irony, and they ring true.

Mother/Daughter Relations

Antoinette grows up as an insecure child in a matriarchy run by her
mother and supported by Christophine. Security comes when Annette
remarries with one of the new people with money, but then patriarchy
takes over. Antoinette is never close to her mother. She believes that
Annette is ashamed of her (WSS, 26). She spends her time with her surrogate mother, Christophine, in the kitchen, because she is afraid of her
real mother, who she believes prefers the company of her retarded
brother to hers. Imperfect though he is, Pierre is a man-child. In a sense
Antoinette reads Annette's giving up on life and retreating into madness after the burning of Coulibri as her ultimate rejection of her daughter. Antoinette, after all, is a "writing daughter" (Kloepfer, 177), like
Rhys herself, in maturity missing and groping for memory of her
deceased mother, seeking understanding in vain, and dealing with the
guilt of an archetypal love/hate relationship.

Characterization

Antoinette's life is a tale of journeys: from the West Indies to England;
from Eden to hell; from freedom, beauty, and power to torture, haggish-

ness, and imprisonment; from childhood to early death. As a creole with all the implications if not the reality of mixed blood (Edward is not sure she is beautiful because she looks differently from the stereotypes of English beauty), she is a flower torn from a culture and a place to which she was born by masculine and imperialistic power. Yet even within the island culture, segmented like most, with racial, class, and economic fissures, she is an "Other" to all: a "white nigger" to blacks, the daughter of a "Martinique" (read: possible black blood) to the parvenu English, and an object of envy and subversion by the jealous mulattos like her "brother" Daniel. Only Christophine loves the lonely child-woman.

As both child and woman, Antoinette has little hope. Her well-meaning, smug English stepfather was unable to prevent the death of her brother, the madness of her mother, and the destruction of her childhood home. When she is in the convent school, she dreams an "evil" dream that she is in hell. In fact, she is heading there. From the beginning she intuitively doubts that life will go well with Edward and she is correct. From childhood on Antoinette knows a terrible truth about humanity: "I went to parts of Coulibri that I had not seen. . . . If the razor grass cut my legs and arms I would think 'It's better than people.' Black ants or red ones . . . rain that soaked me to the skin—once I saw a snake. All better than people. Better. Better, better than people" (*WSS*, 28). Rhys's misanthropy never abated.

Antoinette has one brief moment of joy in her life: the first few days of her honeymoon at Granbois, when, like an Eve and Adam, in a wondrous opening of sexuality, the young couple experience each other in a verdant, primal world, with thoughts of money, power, and control set aside. They are equals, or perhaps she leads. Like a beautiful Caliban, Antoinette initiates Edward into the mysteries of the island and is his guide.

The romantic woman who loves passionately and gives all is extremely vulnerable. In the end there are the inevitable questions: "Why do you hate me? . . . Why do you never come near me? . . . or kiss me, or talk to me? Why do you think I can bear it, what reason do you have for treating me like that?" (*WSS*, 126). Soon she can speak no more. As she is being transported to England, she looks and acts like a ghost (*WSS*, 170). She is silent. Rhys often places signification within the unspoken. As in a scene in a silent film, the heroine has no words of pity for herself.

Edward is the novel's villain, a man who grows more malevolent as the narrative progresses, even though we are seeing the central events of the text through his own eyes and in his own patriarchal words. His love of money, cynicism, distrust, sarcasm, bitterness, falseness, prejudice, and hatred grow as he becomes more secure in his position. At first Rhys treats him sympathetically. He is a younger son to a hard father, who must make his way in the world. Not wanting to be humiliated by a "Creole girl," clearly someone beneath him, he promises Antoinette happiness, and the reader is never sure if his words are duplicitous.

Rhys wants to give Edward the benefit of the doubt. He is not the worst of men. He can be kind and gentle. Ironically, he is kinder to a singed moth than to his wife or any other human: "I took the beautiful creature up in my handkerchief and put it on the railing. . . . I shook the handkerchief gently and it flew away. 'I hope that gay gentleman will be safe' "(WSS, 81). But worked on by his own insecurity and the malevolence of the clever Daniel, he is transformed into the true monster of the story, untrusting in his paranoia and hating everyone.

One of the most distasteful of Edward's characteristics is his racial prejudice. He asks Antoinette, "Why do you hug and kiss Christophine?" She responds, "Why not?" He replies, "I wouldn't hug and kiss them . . . I couldn't" (WSS, 91). His remarks are ringingly ironic, for later, when his lust is up, he is eager to make love to Black Amélie. He assumes the typical male colonist's race hatred of Blacks except when there is a chance to have sex with a Black woman. In the course of the text, Edward comes to associate his creole wife with the black community, and that mentally eases his enslaving of Antoinette, who herself identifies with the Black experience through the treatment she receives from her White master.

Edward is clever, but not deeply intelligent. Daniel outwits and manipulates him easily, and he never realizes what he is losing in destroying Antoinette. Perhaps his greatest fear is fear of his own passion. The self-revealed sexual side of his nature is terrifying to this Victorian man. Yet, in mitigation, Antoinette's stepbrother, Richard Mason, is not totally forthcoming with Edward. Edward is not informed that Annette had gone mad, or that Antoinette's brother Pierre is an imbecile. Yes, Antoinette is the victim of Edward's greed and aggressive patriarchal need for control of a pure, perfect, and obedient woman, but she is also a victim of her own passivity. Putting it simply, Antoinette should and could have followed her intuition and stuck to her rejection of Edward, or she could have taken Christophine's advice and left him. Marriage is not quite slavery, after all. They both would have had happier lives, but that, of course, is not the story.

Christophine is not given a narrative of her own, but she is the third most important character in the text. She "embodies the life force," says Lucy Wilson.[6] She has wisdom and power. She is to be admired in that she is "linked to an older and purer African past" (O'Connor, 209). Christophine is an Obeah priestess and philosopher. She may have even helped Annette to her wealthy marriage, but her powers cannot help Antoinette, perhaps because ultimately the suffering protégé does not believe in her: "How can she know the best thing for me to do, this ignorant, obstinate old negro woman" (WSS, 112). In adopting the White attitude, Antoinette dooms herself. But Christophine does know what, deep down, motivates Edward in driving his wife to madness: "You do that for money? But you wicked like Satan self" (WSS, 161). Christophine represents and practices Obeah; Edward is a Christian, presumably a Protestant. It is his God against her spirits. The battle is for the body and soul of Antoinette and, symbolically, for the soul of the British West Indies. Edward defeats Christophine over Antoinette; the symbolic struggle goes on.

Annette Cosway Mason, Antoinette's mother, is a complex person. She has done the best she can for her fatherless family, even to the point of "selling" herself to Mr. Mason so that her children and she can live a much better life than they have been living since the death of the reprobate Cosway. Her plans go awry. The home is burned, and they are driven from their estate as she is driven out of her mind by the thought of how she has miscalculated and how she has given herself to a man who appeared capable of protecting the family and providing for its needs but proved an inadequate fool. Antoinette recalls her mother screaming at Mason, "Don't touch me. I'll kill you if you touch me. Coward. Hypocrite. I'll kill you" (WSS, 47). Annette is cut off from love and isolated from family and friends. This is the result of an economic-based marriage or, indeed, marriage to an Englishman.

We never learn Mr. Mason's first name. He is so formal an Englishman that it seems he hardly has or needs one. Despite Annette's attack on him, he is no coward. When his family is in danger at Coulibri, he tries to defend them as best he can. When it seems they are all to be killed, he prays and they are saved. He is a supercilious, superior, racist colonial. Although he is generous and he clearly loves his beautiful Annette, he is condescending to her and feels that she is not quite the equal to an English woman. Rhys has consciously decided to portray an archetype with Mason rather than a truly individualized character: the wealthy English capitalist abroad who is just, fair, well-meaning, bigoted, and dangerous in his arrogance. Yes, all of Rhys's characters in this text sadly are marooned in the wide Sargasso Sea.

Narrative Technique

Rhys's narrative technique is different in *Wide Sargasso Sea* in that for the first and only time she writes a novel in which the point of view is not always that of the heroine. In fact it is the stranger and enemy to be, Edward, who narrates the main section of the text. The technique is a surprise, but it is successful because it prevents Antoinette from harrowing the reader with her suffering, thus making it both more real and more general. Furthermore, Edward's narration prevents Rhys from directly justifying her heroine. It is as if the author is allowing the accused to convict himself on his own testimony. Adding Antoinette's and Grace Poole's testimony in the narrative makes *Wide Sargasso Sea* much more of a modernist, impressionist novel (Ashcom, 25). The reader is required to integrate the separate statements and create the full narrative in her or his mind.

Rhys's style is finely honed. It is sparse, direct, and concrete. She allows only what is required for us to understand the plot and accept the most innocent of heroines, who is an unloved girl of little education and less experience, as a tragic figure emblematic of Victorian women and woman as colonial "Other," trapped between two disdainful cultures.

Rhys's artistic triumph in *Wide Sargasso Sea* resides in her ability to devise a story that combines a personal tragedy with a historical debacle during a time of overwhelming social and gender injustice. Plot and dialogue skillfully reveal and support the personal dramas that are truly determined by cultural and social attitudes and values as well as historical events. The reader feels that Antoinette Bertha Cosway Mason Rochester's story could not have been told any other way.

Imagery

Wide Sargasso Sea contains a lush tropical world created by evocative and powerful literal imagery that externalizes the internal conflicts of the protagonist and antagonist. It is a world that is exotic but foreboding to an English sensibility. Upon arriving in the rain on the island where he and Antoinette will spend their honeymoon, Edward observes, "the sad, leaning cocoanut palms, the fishing boats drawn up on the shingly beach, the uneven row of whitewashed huts, and asked the name of the village" (*WSS*, 65). He is told "Massacre." But no one knows who and when.

As the party progresses toward Granbois, "The road climbed upward. On one side the wall of green, on the other a steep drop to the ravine below. We pulled up and looked at the hills, the mountains and the blue-green sea. There was a soft warm wind blowing but I understood why the porter had called it a wild place. Not only wild but menacing. Those hills would close in on you" (*WSS*, 69). But all Edward could verbalize is, "What an extreme green" (*WSS*, 69).

Part two, the central and longest section of the text, contains the best descriptive imagery in the Rhys canon. Clearly she was inspired by her childhood memory and her 1930s trip to recreate the beauty and the natural power of the islands in her one Caribbean novel. Unlike the author's farewell, Edward's is filled with hatred of fauna and flora.

> I was tired of these people. I disliked their laugher and their tears, their flattery and envy, conceit and deceit. And I hated the place. I hated the mountains and the hills, the rivers and the rain. I hated the sunsets of whatever colour. I hated its beauty and its magic and the secret I would never know. I hated its indifference and the cruelty which was a part of its loveliness. Above all I hated her. For she belonged to the magic and the loveliness. She had left me thirsty and all life would be thirst and longing for what I had lost before I found it. (*WSS*, 172)

Edward the Englishman has given up nature, love, and beauty for money, hatred of a poor woman, and the pleasure of torturing her.

Nancy J. Leigh has pointed out the significance of the mirror image in *Wide Sargasso Sea*.[7] For in the patriarchal Victorian world, women survive or perish in proportion to their physical attractiveness, and when that erodes or a husband tires of it, they perish anyway. They are often each other's mirror. We see the fading of Antoinette's mother through the daughter's eyes, and in the end Antoinette's deterioration through Grace Poole's vision (*WSS*, 177). Early on, the widowed Annette is "pretty," so she "still planned and hoped—perhaps she had to every time she passed a looking glass" (*WSS*, 18). The great fear, of course, is aging, but Annette may also be looking for signs that mental strains are appearing on her face.

As cited above, when Antoinette is hit by a stone thrown by her Black companion Tia, and is bleeding, she saw herself "like in a looking glass" (*WSS*, 45). Seeing herself Black is a manifestation of Antoinette's identification with Blacks, the very people who at the moment are oppressing her. She is a self-appointed member of the group that is out to hurt her, a group that has rejected her. Thus she is doubly isolated.

At Granbois Antoinette remembers a visit when she was younger in which, on a hot night, trying to sleep, she sees "two enormous rats, big as cats" in the mirror on the other side of the room (WSS, 82). She is only wearing a chemise and is very frightened. The rats represent her fear of her own budding sexuality and what fate it may bring her here in her mother's place.

When Antoinette is under Grace Poole's supervision and mad, because her husband has bestowed the powerful word "mad" on her, she tells us that there is no mirror in her prison: "there is no looking glass here and I don't know what I am like now. I remember watching myself brush my hair and how my eyes looked back at me. The girl I saw was myself yet not quite myself. Long ago when I was a child and very lonely I tried to kiss her. But the glass was between us" (WSS, 180). She was so lonely that she desperately tried to be her own friend, to love herself, to embrace her spirit, but the material world intervened. Now she does not need a mirror. She has seen her image before. She knows what she looks like. She is her mother now.

The animal images, carrying their thematic burden of helplessness, commence with the early discovery that Annette's horse has been wantonly slain by Blacks, and Antoinette has found the corpse with its "eyes black with flies" (WSS, 18). As stated above, Antoinette believes that all animals are better than people (WSS, 28). Rats and snakes also inhabit Granbois and its environs. Eden is far from perfect. Christophine thinks that the tea "English madams drink" is "yellow horse piss," while her coffee is "bull's blood" (WSS, 85). Of course the immolation of poor Coco the parrot, whose wings have been clipped by Mr. Mason so that he cannot fly away and avoid the flames, is the single most powerful image in the text: symbolically, the horrifying death of a beautiful innocent, and the death of innocence itself.

Conclusion

Jean Rhys began writing *Wide Sargasso Sea* in her late forties. The story incubated for over two decades in her unconscious mind. In her old age, after her rediscovery, Rhys's friends and editors squeezed one more novel out of her. It is her finest work. In depicting an innocent woman's total disintegration in a system of empire in which she is denied a respectful place (Emery, 429), this last text sums up Rhys's rebellion against the male-colonized worlds of money, art, and sexuality.

Ultimately, *Wide Sargasso Sea* is a story about a love that turns to an unequal contest for imperialistic control and a tale of passion that fails to overcome cultural, class, and racial differences. It is about the cruelty humans are capable of inflicting on those they are supposed to love and care for. It is also about the opposing ways "in which human beings perceive the world, each other and themselves" (Staley, 120).

In her creative imagination Jean Rhys revisited Dominica and a great novel she had read many years before that had offended her because of its treatment of a creole woman. She combined these experiences to produce a woman's Gothic nightmare unmatched in twentieth-century British literature.

Chapter Eight

Tigers Are Better-Looking and *Sleep It Off, Lady*

Jean Rhys wrote short stories at the beginning of her literary career in the 1920s before *Quartet,* during the 1930s, and near the end of her career in the 1960s. She did not grow and develop much as a writer of short fiction. She seemed to feel as if stories were exercises and novels were "writing" (Angier, 341). What changed with time were her subjects, and, naturally, the heroine of the stories grew older. That heroine is invariably a loner, an outcast, and a victim. A. C. Morrell states that in her stories, "Rhys's world-view is uncompromising: the making of scapegoats is society's first and necessary evil."[1] Rhysland in short fiction is populated with two divisions of people: the respectable and the "Others." Rhys's heroines, like the author herself, stood with the "Others."

Tigers Are Better-Looking

Tigers Are Better-Looking (1968) contains eight stories that were first published in periodicals and short story collections in the early 1960s and ten stories reprinted from *The Left Bank.* Significantly, the two most powerful stories, "Till September Petronella" and "Tigers Are Better-Looking," were first written in the late 1930s (Angier, 341) but not published at that time. Along with "Sleep It Off, Lady" they are her finest works of short fiction.

"Till September Petronella" came out in *The London Magazine* in 1960. It is the story of an actress, Petronella Grey, who has an invitation for a holiday in the country with Andrew Marston, a painter and avuncular good friend, as well as with another couple, the music critic Julian Oakes and his girlfriend, the sharp-tongued and independent model Frankie Morell. The latter couple bicker continually, and their battling and attempts to draw Petronella into the conflict cause her to run away from the unpleasant group. She is picked up by a farmer, who propositions her crudely and treats her in a patronizing way, but his protective actions and attitudes are welcome, and she is able to return alone to

London, where again she is picked up. The young man, Melville, and Petronella walk in Hyde Park and dine. She tells him how her dramatic career has stagnated and later requests an expensive gift from him, the same gift the farmer had hinted at providing when he said farewell at the train and "I'll see you in September, Petronella."[2]

Melville is turned off by Petronella's sudden materialism, and he leaves, saying, "I'll do my best, but I'm not one of them plutocrats, you know" (*Tigers*, 38). She warns him not to come back without the gift. He quickly departs, echoing the farmer, "All right, I'll see you in September, Petronella" (*Tigers*, 39), and she is alone again in the small room where the story commenced.

Petronella has some power as a young and beautiful woman, but, unlike the assertive Frankie, she does not know how to use it. She expects to play up to male vanity and submit (Leigh, 280). Her friend Marston is a gentle, considerate man, but he, too, is manipulated and abused by others, like his friend Oakes. He cannot maintain the relationship with Petronella because, paradoxically, he lacks the very masculine attributes she is attracted to but is always taken advantage of by. In "Till September Petronella" Rhys offers evidence that women must not be soft and malleable, yet even when they harden protectively, they cannot escape the debilitation of ingrained sexism.

"The Day They Burned the Books" was first published in *The London Magazine* in 1960. Set in the Caribbean, a Black widow of a White man who abused her but loved books "punishes" him after his death when she burns his books, to the consternation and grief of two children, a boy and a girl who also love books and are perplexed at the irrationality of the vengeance.

"Let Them Call It Jazz" was first published in *The London Magazine* in 1962. A Caribbean Black seamstress living in London, Selina Davis, experiences racial prejudice, discrimination, and unequal treatment from her landlady, neighbors, the police, and the judicial system. Despite abuse and arrest, her inherent good nature and optimism allow her to endure and survive. A Caribbean song she sings is noted and sold. Given five pounds, she does what makes her happy: "I buy myself a dusty pink dress with the money" (*Tigers*, 67). A particular success of the story is Rhys's presentation of a West Indian dialect.

"Tigers Are Better-Looking" was first published in *The London Magazine* in 1962. The story depicts London Bohemian life in the 1930s as hard and vicious. Severn, an Australian journalist, is making the rounds of Soho with two young women, Maidie and Heather. They go to the

Jim-Jam club on Heather's recommendation and because she seems to be employed in bringing in customers. There he is continually cheated in the admission charge and through the drinks ordered. Severn gets into a scrap with a waiter and is bounced. The altercation continues outside, where Severn knocks down a waiter and is enjoying himself for a moment. The waiter gets up and hits poor Maidie, who can only swear back (*Tigers*, 76). Then Severn is hurled into the gutter by three men, and the police arrive to arrest him and Maidie. Afterwards he is insulted when Maidie states that they are too old "to enjoy a thing like this," and he drops her (*Tigers*, 81).

While the good-hearted Maidie has gotten nothing from the experience except a bruised face and body aches from being kicked, Severn is a writer, and he has a story. London is a place where one "is surrounded by a pack of timid tigers waiting to spring the moment anybody is in trouble or hasn't any money. *But tigers are better-looking, aren't they?*" (*Tigers*, 68).

"Outside the Machine" was first published in *Winter's Tales* (London: Macmillan, 1960). The story somewhat mitigates Rhys's antipathy toward other women and belief in an inherent, almost deadly competition within the sex. In a Versailles clinic a penniless, despairing young woman named Inez is about to be discharged too soon because beds are needed for new patients. An old patient, Mrs. Tavernier, gives her money to get by on for a while. Inez is surprised. "She had never taken money from a woman before. She did not like women, she had always told herself, or trust them" (*Tigers*, 105). They kiss, and for the first time a Rhys heroine comes to realize that "sometimes it's peaceful" in old age (*Tigers*, 106). The Rhys heroine is slowly making peace with women as well as the aging process.

"The Lotus" was first published in *Art and Literature* in 1967. In the story an old, unkempt, lonely, alcoholic poet, Lotus Heath, who lives in a filthy basement flat, imposes on her upstairs neighbors, Christine and Ronnie Miles. Christine despises Lotus and resents her taking up Ronnie's time, drinking his whiskey, and winning his sympathy. Later, when Lotus runs naked in the street and is arrested, Ronnie cowardly denies that he knows her well, and the other tenants in the house do not help the police either. No one will take any responsibility for an old woman in trouble. There is no community compassion. Ronnie distracts himself from any possible pangs of guilt when Lotus is taken away by making love to his wife: "a lovely child. So lovely he had to tell her how lovely she was, and start kissing her" (*Tigers,* 119). Her soul is not lovely, and one day she, too, will be old and perhaps alone.

"A Solid House" was first published in *Voices* (London: Michael Joseph, 1963). It is set in the London Blitz of 1940–41. Miss Spearman, the unpleasant old manager of the rooming house, sells second-hand clothes and dabbles in spiritualism. She pressures lodgers to buy hideous garments from her to supplement her income. The sensitive and depressed tenant Teresa is flirted with by an older tenant, Captain Roper, but the relationship is aborted when she laughs at the wrong place in one of his stories.

Ironically, in a city where scores of people are being blown to bits each night, Teresa tries to commit suicide and fails, but she feels that she really has died anyway. She would like to confide in Miss Spearman, but the older woman is not interested in any life but her own. Miss Spearman wants Teresa to go to a seance with her, but Teresa is not ready to join with the other dead. She needs rest and her "little sleep" first (*Tigers*, 137).

The house may be solid in a city where structures are being destroyed daily, but the society is not. Each person lives selfishly within her or his fantasies and for her or his needs. Individuals are always alone, even when they think they are not. They do not really communicate; they talk at each other. Community does not exist, nor does brotherhood, sisterhood, family ties, or the bonds of lovers. After all, the world is always at war.

"The Sound of the River" was first published in *Art and Literature* in 1966. In the story a woman who has been ill and dependent on her husband wakes up to find him dead in their bed. Time seems to stop for her as she tries to get to a phone in a neighbor's house, but he is away and she must break in to call a doctor who, later, wonders suspiciously why it took so long to reach him. In the end she is listening to the sound of the nearby river. It grows louder. The river symbolizes life flowing by and collecting human debris. It has come into the room with her (*Tigers*, 144). Incidentally, Rhys is subtextually explaining the circumstances of the death of her second husband (Angier, 428).

The precision writing and acid tone of the newer stories in *Tigers Are Better-Looking* indicate that Rhys's fictive skills bridged novel and story. Furthermore, she continued to process experience into art.

Sleep It Off, Lady

Sleep It Off, Lady (1976) contains 16 pieces, of which 7 were previously published in periodicals in the late 1960s and early 1970s. The stories are about outcasts, loners, and women who are generally excluded from the position of active, decision-making participants in society. These are invisible people, except when the establishment wishes to make trouble for them. They are not actors, but acted upon.

"Pioneers, Oh, Pioneers" first appeared in the London *Times* under the title "Dear Darling Mr. Ramage." The story is set on a Caribbean island, presumably Dominica, in 1899. Seen through the eyes of Rosalie, a kind doctor's sensitive daughter (like Dr. Williams and his daughter Ella Gwendoline), a young Englishman, Mr. Ramage comes to the island not to become rich but to find peace. He marries a Black woman, grows eccentric, and is hounded into suicide by the community. In the end Rosalie tries to write a letter to the dead man, who was so misunderstood and badly treated by everyone except Dr. Cox. The child cries and falls asleep, and her mother throws the unfinished letter out of the window, where the breeze takes it up and bounces it "purposely down the street. As if it knew exactly where it was going."[3]

"Goodbye Marcus, Goodbye Rose" was first published in *The New Yorker*. Set in Dominica, an old English soldier, Captain Cardew, molests Phoebe, a 12-year-old girl who is transfixed by his stories of love and violent sex. The convent-educated child is never again able to think of herself as good or pure and is convinced, partly by the attitudes and innuendoes of other adults, that it was her fault that her molester acted as he did and destroyed the innocence of her thought, because he was reacting to the corruption that was already in her. "She learns that as a female she will be blamed for what men do" (Leigh, 281). No longer can she dream of a trousseau, marriage, and naming her children "Jack, Marcus, and Rose" (*Sleep*, 30). The story is one of a tragic end of innocence in which a child victim is blamed by others and blames herself for the beastly behavior of an adult who not only fondles her breasts but also rapes her mind and spirit.

"The Bishop's Feast" is a brief story depicting the humorless pomposity of men, like bishops, who hold power over women, like nuns, and never can forgive being laughed at for even a brief moment. "Heat," first published in *The New Yorker*, is set at the time of the great catastrophe of the eruption of Mont Pelée on the Island of Martinique, where 40,000 humans were killed in the destruction of the town of St. Pierre on 8 May 1902. A child on Dominica begins a lifelong fascination with the disaster. People begin to blame the victims, claiming the town was wicked because it had "not only a theatre, but an opera house" (*Sleep*, 41). When the child grows up she comes to know "it wasn't like that" (*Sleep*, 41).

"Fishy Waters," the longest story in *Sleep It Off, Lady*, is set in Roseau, Dominica, in the 1890s. In it a disreputable, hard-drinking English carpenter, Jimmy Longa, is accused of badly beating a naked Black girl child and is convicted and driven off the island on circumstantial evidence and because the White community wants this unacceptable White man out of its hair. In the end, the wife of the star witness against Longa comes to realize that, most likely, it was her husband who committed the atrocity. Once more, the wealthy and the powerful go unpunished and the powerless are the scapegoats.

"Overture and Beginners Please" is set in Cambridge, England, where a displaced girl from the West Indies is spending Christmas holiday almost alone in her boarding school because her one English relative, an aunt, has not invited her. She is cold and lonely, and she wonders, "What is going to become of me? Why am I here at all?" (*Sleep*, 70). But she has been a hit in the school play, and her friend Myrtle convinces her that she is "a born actress." She persuades her father to let her prepare for entrance into Tree's school for actors, but after a term there her father dies and she becomes a chorus girl over family objections. She goes on tour and learns to obscure her background in order to get along and get by (*Sleep*, 77).

The next story, "Before the Deluge," picks up the same West Indian girl's tale. She is now a full-fledged actress. The story is a character sketch of her older, patronizing chum Daisy, who is given to temperamental flare-ups and "fainting," an episode of which ends the friendship. "On Not Shooting Sitting Birds" was first published in *The New Yorker*. In it the young woman persona of these autobiographical stories has a date with an attractive Englishman who she hopes will make love to her, in anticipation of which she invests in sexy, expensive underwear, a "milanese silk chemise and drawers" (*Sleep*, 90). But in trying to impress the upper-class Englishman with her West Indian background, she commits a verbal blunder, not knowing the conventions of an English shooting party, and the date is a bust. But she'll use the underwear another time.

"Kikimora" was first published in *The New Yorker*. Kikimora is a black cat who scratches Baron Mumtael, a guest of Elsa, who has cooked a fine dinner for him and her husband Stephen. Nervous, Elsa has drunk too much whiskey, and she takes great offense at the Baron's condescension and male chauvinism, to the point that when the guest leaves she shocks her husband by cutting up the suit she was wearing: "I'm destroying my feminine charm. . . . I thought I'd make a nice quick clean job of it" (*Sleep*, 99).

"Night Out 1925" and "The Chevalier of the Place Blanche" are set in Paris. The latter is "a much-adapted" translation of a story by Edouard de Nève. In the former a young girl on a date with a parsimonious Englishman is taken to a night club in which women perform sexual acts with each other for a price. The date is a fiasco partly because the Englishman is so cheap. The couple need to escape the fury of the performers, and the Englishman, Gilbert, hands his date, Suzy, his wallet with instructions to give the girls a very small tip. Unbeknownst to him, she takes out two large bills and gives them to the two performers they had previously selected. She is moved to sympathy by the hard life of the women in the club. Outside, Gilbert, learning that he has inadvertently been generous, puts Suzy on a bus to go home alone. Here is another failure of a heterosexual relationship because of the different perspectives, values, and sympathies of women and men.

"The Chevalier of the Place Blanche" "is intimately acquainted with the police of three countries" (*Sleep*, 113). A native of Montmartre is dining in Montparnasse when a beautiful English girl, a demimondaine, picks him up. He sees her on several occasions and then invites her to his room, which he prepares for seduction, but she puts him off as he tries to take her in his arms. Nevertheless, she asks him to go to Madrid with her, but he informs her truthfully that he cannot because he has embezzled and spent a large sum of money from a tourist office he is employed in, and if he does not return the sum the next day, he will be in very serious trouble. The girl, Margaret, offers to give him the money if he will go away with her. But his "masculine pride" is wounded (*Sleep*, 121). He will not be taken for a gigolo or an Apache. He turns her down and they go their separate ways, even though they need each other very badly. Men cannot accept generosity and a reversal of traditional power roles, even when benign, in a heterosexual relationship.

"The Insect World" was first published in Britain in *The Sunday Times Magazine* and in the United States in *Mademoiselle*. Like "A Solid House" in *Tigers Are Better-Looking,* it takes place during the London Blitz, where Audrey, a frightened, single woman, almost 29, worries about survival without a husband after she reaches age 30. She dreads growing old, and has been embarrassed by a young female clerk in a dress shop who treated her as if she were an older matron (*Sleep*, 129). Audrey hates older women, but when she sees an elderly woman physically mistreated, she momentarily identifies with her. Audrey has been haunted by the thought of insects and begins to think that people "were insects" (*Sleep*, 132). She is losing her self-control, perhaps under the pressure of the war and the bombing, and when her friend Monica says in the cliché way, "All right, old girl," the enraged Audrey rushes at her with clenched fists, shouting, "Damn your soul to everlasting hell *don't call me that.*" (*Sleep*, 136). Growing older is hell, torture, and death for the Rhys heroine.

"Rapunzel, Rapunzel" and "Who Knows What's up in the Attic?" are based on and were written during the despairing period in Rhys's life prior to her rediscovery. She called them "horror stories" (Angier, 609). In "Rapunzel, Rapunzel" a woman whose home is in Devon has been hallucinating in a London hospital, but she is then discharged to a convalescent home, where in the next bed, she sees an old lady with "long, silvery white, silky" hair that she brushes (*Sleep*, 140). A man's barber misunderstands the old lady's instructions to trim the ends of her hair and instead cuts most of it off and destroys the last element of her identity as an attractive woman. The old woman is devastated because it is too late for her glorious hair to grow back, and she sickens and is taken away in the night, presumably to die. The persona refuses to accept what has happened and thinks, "She'll probably get perfectly well. Her hair will grow again and will soon look pretty" (*Sleep*, 144). But, "unreasonably," words repeat in her head: "Rapunzel, Rapunzel, let down your hair?" (*Sleep*, 144). It is a despairing person's call for death. The moral is that a woman should hold on to her feminine identity for as long as she is able. For the author that is the only identity that counts.

In "Who Knows What's up in the Attic?" a lonely older woman initially feels happy and secure because of the attentions of a young male stranger from Holland who looks like Mogdigliani (*Sleep*, 151). But when he tells her of the troubles in his marriage, she is reminded of sad events in her own youth, so she breaks off the relationship abruptly, fearing the return of debilitating depression. As Rhys is writing the last of her short fiction, she is practically writing autobiography, taking episodes from her life and shaping them into readable, interesting, and moving vignettes with a sympathetic spin on events and personal actions.

"Sleep It Off, Lady," a particularly fine story, was first published in the *New Review*. In it an old unmarried woman, Miss Verney, wants to tear down an unattractive, galvanized iron shed on her property, but she cannot get someone to tear it down for her. She hallucinates that "a fierce and dangerous animal lived there" (*Sleep*, 160). The description of the decrepit shed is vivid: "the paint had worn off the once-black galvanized iron. Now it was a greenish colour. Part of the roof was loose and flapped noisily in windy weather and a small gate off its hinges leaned up against the entrance" (*Sleep*, 160).

Inside the shed, "Nails festooned with rags protruded from the only wooden rafter. Nettles flourished in one corner" (*Sleep*, 160). The old shed stands for the old lady's depressed self-perception. It is worn-out like an old body. It takes up space and is useless. It houses a dangerous animal. No one will take the shed or her off the land.

Later, moving a large stone, she collapses in the trash from a spilled dust bin. She calls to passing people but is unheard. A nasty child stops to talk to her, but instead of helping her, the girl assumes Miss Verney to be drunk, and says "Sleep it off, lady" (*Sleep*, 171). Like a woman in a Beckett play, she is left in the garbage heap by her neighbors. Found the next day and taken to a hospital, she dies from her ordeal. The stated cause of death is "heart failure," but no one really knew that her heart had not failed. It had broken.

The last, short piece in *Sleep It Off, Lady*, "I Used to Live Here Once," is set in the West Indies and has a spirit who does not realize that she is dead, or who is merely a woman old enough to be "unseen," trying unsuccessfully to communicate with some young people. She says, "I lived where you live and as you live. Remember me."

In *Sleep It Off, Lady* Rhys revisits all her places of sojourn: Dominica, London, Paris, Devon, and back to the West Indies. She also revisits her life from youth to old age and projects a poignant spiritual moment after death.

At any age it is always dangerous to be a woman in Jean Rhys's stories. Fighting back for her protagonists, she used her last fiction to get a little revenge on neighbors, doctors, social workers, and others whom she saw as abusers, users, and manipulators. But the stories are vital, moving, poignant, and enjoyable whether or not the reader is aware of their darker purpose or their biographical sources.

Chapter Nine
Autobiographical Writing

Jean Rhys produced two autobiographical works: *My Day* (1975) and *Smile Please: An Unfinished Autobiography* (1979). Her autobiographical writings were motivated by the urging of friends and by her desire to answer and correct many things that over the years others had said about her life (Athill: *Smile*, 3). It is sad that Rhys started too late and did not have enough time or strength left to write a full-fledged autobiography. One can only speculate that the work would have been scathingly fascinating and almost as popular as *Wide Sargasso Sea.* Instead fans of Jean Rhys must be satisfied with the fragmented memoirs of *My Day* and *Smile Please,* and of course, Carole Angier's splendid biography.

Carol R. Hagley notes that "When she wrote *My Day* Jean Rhys still possessed that spirit of defiance that is necessary for survival."[1] She was fighting to maintain, perhaps regain, control of the story of her life and art. Mistakes had been written about her and incorrect implications made by such authors as Arthur Mizener, the biographer of Ford Madox Ford. Also, she wanted those who were, are, and would be interested in the writer's life to know that she was not really the Rhys "heroine." She was Jean Rhys.

My Day

My Day (1975) contains three short memoirs. The title piece, "My Day," which first appeared in the U.S. and British *Vogue* in 1975, tells of an old woman's diurnal activities in her Devon cottage: waking, reading, cooking, resting, sleeping, and doing a little shopping. She talks of beauty in the animal world, "Lions, cats, horses . . . hummingbirds, butterflies, even goldfish,"[2] and she paraphrases another writer of her generation, Stevie Smith, a kindred spirit who, as a woman, had struggled for a creative existence and who seemed to love animals more than people: "It's all very well to talk about the beauty of the human body, but I can think of a whole lot of other things more beautiful" (*MD*, 8). Significantly

Rhys has given up despairing over aging and the loss of youthful physical beauty.

Coral Ann Howells has pointed out that Rhys's essentially uneventful account of her daily life ends "like a classic modernist short story with a moment of revelation" (Howells, 149). The persona creates a demonic fantasy that is "pure domestic Gothic" (Howells, 149).

> When I first came here, I always left my door open because, after all, I've nothing to steal. . . . Now I always lock up through thinking sometimes of that very frightening ghost story about the solitary woman who has just turned the key and shot the bolt for the night when she hears a voice behind her saying: "Now we are alone together." (*MD*, 10)

Surely it is death who cannot be locked out. Wisely, "My Day" was incorporated as the concluding piece of *Smile Please*.

"Invitation to the Dance" is a memoir of childhood games and songs in Roseau. In "Close Season for the Old?" Rhys again indicates that she has learned to live "with the consequences" of old age (*MD*, 17). She pleads for tolerance for the old and asks that they may live out their lives "without interference, malice or ridicule." (*MD*, 18)

Smile Please

The posthumously published *Smile Please* (1979) is a collection of brief memoirs divided into two parts: "Smile Please," containing 16 pieces relating to Rhys's childhood in Dominica, until she leaves at the age of 16; and "It Began to Grow Cold," primarily containing 12 pieces about her early life as a chorus girl in England and her days in Paris. In the latter section Rhys, as her own subject, grows cold in emigrating from sunny Dominica to Europe, but Rhys as autobiographer grows cold as incapacity and death approach, preventing her from finishing the difficult, painful task of the final writing. As autobiography, the text is too fragmented, but as the recollections of a great writer in her mid eighties, it is very interesting and rewarding even if some of the reminiscences are contrary to known facts.

Rhys shares her recollections of her mother and father, nurses and friends, places she visited, a carnival, her early love of reading, the development of religious feelings, learning about sex, her feelings at leaving her island, obtaining work as a chorus girl in London, the "gypsy" life, marriage and Paris life in "The Roaring Twenties" among the expatriates. Then Rhys leaps over a chasm of some 25 years to her last years in the cottage in Devon.

With unmitigated honesty she reveals her hates. John Updike states that "this negative emotion gives a macabre tinge to *Smile Please.*"[3] But one cannot forget that Rhys believed that neither the world nor people had treated her very well. As a child she hated the way the mirror told her how she looked. She hated her father with a short haircut, as well as a photo of her mother showing her young and attractive. Later she hated the unknown people who knocked down the cross over her father's grave before her return to Dominica in 1936. She hated the London Zoo and landladies of course, and so much else. Unfortunately, with the experience of seeing her father's grave desecrated, she thinks, "I can hate too" (*SP*, 59), and given the population of Dominica, the implication may be that she can hate Blacks, too. She now claims that it was Meta, her black nurse, "who didn't like me much anyway" (*SP*, 20), who "had shown me a world of fear and distrust, and I am still in that world" (*SP*, 24).

In the convent school Rhys admired a beautiful girl of color and tried to talk to her: "Without speaking she turned and looked at me. I knew irritation, bad temper, the 'Oh, go away' look; this was different. This was hatred—impersonal, implacable hatred. . . . I never tried to be friendly with any coloured girls again . . . They hate us. We are hated" (*SP*, 39).

Reading was an early passion for Rhys, but the activity annoyed Meta, who tried to frighten her charge: "If all you read so much, you know what will happen to you? Your eyes will drop out and they will look at you from the page." But the child "went on reading" (*SP*, 21). Rhys speaks about starting to write at 19, after the crash of her first love affair, and then proceeds to rush over the territory of the early novels. That very creative part of her life is what is most neglected in *Smile Please* and most missed by readers.

As a child Jean Rhys believed that her mother cared less for her and gave her less time than she gave her siblings, but she loved her mother and missed her terribly after leaving Dominica. They never again established a close relationship, even when the widow Minna Rees Williams moved to England. The "cathexis between mother and daughter," says Adrienne Rich, "is the great unwritten story."[4] Given that the dominant discourse was partial to the Freudian relationships of mother and son, father and daughter, and the archetypal conflict of brothers, it is not surprising that the mother/daughter relationship, the great architectonic of familial continuity, is absent or muted in Rhys's work, but her appreciation of the power of motherhood and the emotional bond with her own mother is evident.

A child in the convent school Rhys attended is asked by the mother superior, "Who made you?" The child does not answer "God," but instead "persisted obstinately in saying, 'My mother!' " The nun replies, "no dear, that's not the answer. Now think—who made you?" The "stolid" girl replies, "My mother," and the nun "banished her from the class" (*SP*, 64). Unlike the nun, the little girl will not be exploited by the power of the "Father," and Rhys commends her for it.

Smile Please begins with the vignette "Smile Please," in which the author, 16 and wearing her birthday dress, is having her photograph taken and is told by the photographer to "smile please" and look "not quite so serious" (*SP*, 13). The text goes on to become a series of album photos until an old woman appears. The word pictures are serious, with the subject often frowning, but then the author saw her life as serious, perhaps heroic and tragic, and the frown was the right facial expression for her.

It is best for the reader to consider *Smile Please* as an assemblage of fascinating recollections by a brilliant woman in her mid eighties who had lived a modern odyssey and was approaching the end of her life rather than as a factual, biographical tool. The text tells us as much about what the elderly Jean Rhys had become as it does about how Ella Gwendoline Rees Williams evolved into a major modernist writer. But then the making of an artist is always a mystery, and the creative road runs largely through the night.

Chapter Ten

"The Best Living English Novelist": Summation and Achievement

In one of those landmark *New York Times Book Review* pieces that alter, restore, or renew literary reputations, the poet A. Alvarez wrote on 17 March 1974, in regard to the paperback publication of Rhys's earlier novels, "Although her range is narrow, sometimes to the point of obsession, there is no one else now writing who combines such emotional penetration and formal artistry or approaches her unemphatic, unblinking truthfulness."[1] He titled his review "The Best Living English Novelist," and at the age of 84 Jean Rhys was a famous, best-selling author for the first time in her life.

It has recently been noted by Noel Annan that the most interesting British novelists of this century "were women: Ivy Compton-Burnett, Rosamond Lehmann, Iris Murdoch, Jean Rhys, Stevie Smith and Muriel Spark."[2] Indeed it can be argued that women novelists like Rhys obtained real freedom of expression as the true twentieth century began, that is, in the year 1914, when the initial great male mass suicide of the century commenced.

Annan chose to omit Virginia Woolf, arguably the greatest of British woman novelists of the twentieth century, from his list of premier woman writers in the period, placing her, incorrectly perhaps, among the Edwardians she disdained. Rhys was only eight years younger than Woolf. Except that both presented their heroines from the inside out and sometimes employed the stream-of-consciousness technique, their work is enormously different as, indeed, their lives were. Rhys was as far removed from the sensibilities, affluence, assurance, and acceptance of the Bloomsbury circle as a writer could be. Female characters in the world of Woolf's fiction were struggling to create a harmonious and more just society, especially as that society treated and respected women. Woolf's female characters echewed male protection. Rhys's women craved it because the Rhys heroine literally struggled to survive, and there was no possibility of survival for her without (or tragically even with) complicity in the male power structure. Yet today many scholars and critics place Rhys as second only to Woolf as the most significant woman novelist of the high modernist period. A scholar-critic can only be amazed and fascinated by the amount of scholarship and criticism produced concerning Rhys's five novels and three collections of stories, and all this about a writer forgotten for a third of her adult life.

Jean Rhys as Rebel

Jean Rhys was a rebel in her art and in her life. She shocked the bourgeois reading public and the publishers who pandered to it by daring to present women of the demimonde as sensitive, feeling, wronged human beings who nevertheless wanted and sometimes enjoyed sex (and drink); who fought their losing battles with aging and exploitative society alone; who asked no quarter; who comprehended men for what they possessed, what they did, and what they were; and, when occasionally they could, used them in kind. In the Rhys canon there are women who are uneducated, who survive for a while on the power of their youthful looks, who are apolitical, who barely seem to know that a war may be on or over, who are not longing to be homemakers and mothers, who are not brilliant, and who have no deep philosophical thoughts and truths to impart to us. In other words they are just women and just people who, like most of us, live a brief while in this world and pass with little notice.

In these respects the Jean Rhys heroine is unique in modernist literature. Rhys never attempts to create a specialness for her heroines. Like Willy Loman, their distinction lies in their representative ordinariness. They are a collective symbol: alienated woman in patriarchal Western society of the early twentieth century. Her female equivalent may only be found in eighteenth-century satire like Daniel Defoe's *Moll Flanders*. Rhys's personal vision of alienation, desperation, and despair was in her time approached in other women's texts only by Christina Stead, the other great rediscovered colonial woman novelist of the twentieth century.

Rhys is also a rebel in that she seems to have intuitively believed that women are always on trial, that they need to defend themselves in some way, and that one way is by negation, that is, to overtly and subversively attack society's social codes and structures of meaning.[3] Thus we are presented with the demimondaine heroines and their amoral values.

Additionally there is the virtual absence from the texts of male-dominated and fabricated church and state institutions, except for the convent school, which, of course, is run and taught by women.

Although a rebel, Rhys was not a revolutionary. She stood alone, an individual who, after adolescence, seldom trusted man or woman. She did not identify herself as a feminist or anything else political. Outwardly she appeared to accept the male-created role of woman as the purchasable Other, a passive victim, a sometimes silly thing longing to live in her doll's house, a negative and jealous person, evil-fated, a creature of self-indulgence, self-pity, indolence, weariness, and even sleepiness. But inwardly, silently (except in her rages), Rhys struggled against the stereotypes. It was the process of writing that helped Rhys to learn from her life and give voice to the injustices, exploitation, use, and misuse women endured in her time. The subtextual mode is indignation. The action is nullification. Catharsis distilled from pity, terror, and anger is proffered. The final powerful narrative authority is hers.

V. S. Naipaul understands and best states that "out of her fidelity to her experience . . . Jean Rhys thirty or forty years ago identified many of the themes that engage us today: isolation, an absence of society or community, the sense of things falling apart, dependence, loss. Her achievement is very grand. Her books may serve current causes, but she is above causes."[4]

Although she did not like to be alone, Rhys was very secretive about her inner life, and her writing was a product and reflection of that life. Thus she was reluctant to publish, to share that life with friends or strangers who might prove critical. Constant rewriting gave her an opportunity to explain to herself what had happened to her in her life and, in the process, the chance to alter, change, or cover up what had transpired but was too terrible for her to remember as it had truly occurred. Within her inner self she also found her revenge on men and patriarchy, never considering that she could have joined with other women for mutual protection and to attempt to obtain justice. She was an excluded person, excluded by gender, class, and her colonial background. She came near to accepting that exclusion, and fortunately for English letters, she used it for her art.

Rhys's Women

The world of Rhys's fiction is one of cafés, boardinghouse rooms, mirrors, and beds, spaces generally "independent of the surrounding literary zeitgeist" (Kloepfer, 64). It is as a novelist that Rhys will be remembered, and her novels are women's books. On the other hand, Rhys's women are most often marginal people, sometimes displaced from their Caribbean home and always outsiders to "women's traditional domestic world" as they trespass on "masculine public territory" (Emery, "Politics," 418). They are parasitic and often passive, more mannequin than they realize. These women pass through men's lives as incidents. They are professional guests. Witness "the hotel rooms. the bills paid by occasional lovers, the meals never prepared at home but consumed in restaurants in situations that emphasize the political dependence on the one who pays the bill" (Borinsky, 299). In the end they are alienated and depressed. The women pay a terrible psychological and physical price for their accommodation in the patriarchal world.

"Specifically, her novels involve a triad of concerns: sexuality, money, and social position, each a potential source of power and consequently of vulnerability."[5] Above all Rhys knew and could express what it was to be a woman. And she chose to work on a small stage built of a woman's heart and body on which she sang of love, betrayal, and anger. Sadly her heroines achieve only disillusionment. All undertake a voyage "into darkness and nothingness" (Curtis, 148).

Rhys was a costive creator, because writing forced her to remember unhappy events she wanted to forget. But what else was there for her to write about, to express her creativity with? She knew so little and she knew so much. She wrote out of her body. The work was exposure, like compulsive prostitution. It was only after a long quietus that Rhys could arrive at and confront a subject, indeed revisit one, and objectify it somewhat by placing time and distance between herself and the main character's pain. But creativity is also pleasure for an artist: the development of style, the breathing of life into a medium, the satisfaction of the product. And Rhys could return to the legend of her death and resurrection "time and time again with rueful glee" (Howells, 1).

Rhys would not let herself be labeled as a feminist (Howells, 11), but she has been acknowledged as a significant contributor to the developing canon of feminist literature because she so clearly depicts the degree of exploitation and domination many early twentieth-century women were subject to within a power structure they did not make and could not change. Like millions of women in her time, she chose public complicity and reserved subversion for her inner self and then her writing. Both her life and her work were simultaneously creative and destructive. She wore, wrote about, and wrote through the masks of makeup, attractive clothing, partying, drinking, and ruinous behavior, but Rhys's revealed inner voice is the voice of women's pain. Feminist literary critics see in Rhys's novels the story of the search for the lost mother, the one who abandoned her daughter, denied access to the maternal body, and who may have been hated by the child. It is an unspoken story but one coded by the employment of "sounds and images outside (androcentric) discourse: mothers, babies, blood; chants, singing, shouts; eyes, paintings, hallucinations; oceans, moons, floods, and flame. Back through infancy, madness, childbirth, riddles, curses, and song" (Kloepfer, 177).

Style

As a stylist Rhys was beholden to other modernist writers, women and men. She shared the stream-of-consciousness technique with many, including Virginia Woolf and Dorothy Richardson, who both used it effectively to "impart the inner workings of the mind of . . . female protagonists."[6]

Rhys shared her direct, unembellished, nonmetaphorical prose style with Hemingway and Ford, preferring metonymy as symbol over metaphor. These modernists focused almost exclusively on the empirical world (Ashcom, 19), and the environment, like a prophetic character or Eliot's objective correlative, foreshadows dark events in a character's destiny and impinges on her life.

Like other modernists, Rhys wrote about the uglier, seamier side of life and the loneliness of existence. She incorporated film technique in her writing: fade-outs, quick cuts, long shot and close-up descriptions, and storytelling by sequence. "Like Hemingway she presented characters unwilling to engage in, or incapable of, analysis or philosophical speculation. Rootless and sensual, they act primarily on whim, suggesting by their narrow focus on the drives for sex, drink, and temporary companionship a fearful attitude toward a world either meaningless or threatening. Their private selves are fragile and easily hurt" (Ashcom, 17–18). And like in Hemingway, Isherwood, and even Graham Greene, Jean Rhys establishes a character/author relationship seemingly built with interchangeable parts.

On Men

The world created in Rhys's fiction is one corrupted by men. She sees modern women as controlled and exploited almost as much as Victorian

women were. The Victorian Rochester's manipulation and exploitation
of Antoinette are different from Heidler's of Marya only in degree and
method. Both, and most other Rhys men, objectify and commodify
women. But men also lose out and are cheated because, especially for
them, the basis of male/female relations, particularly marriage, is always
economic. In a society in which exploitation of class, race, ethnicity, and
age occur regularly, why would one expect gender relations to be different? Patriarchal society may have turned women into burdens for men
to bear, but nevertheless they are burdens, and thus abuse, sexual
exploitation, and general misogyny in and by men may be based on
what Helen Nebeker calls "the unconscious sense of perpetual economic
obligation" (Nebeker, 12). Indeed, love, sex, and companionship as economic transactions degrade both parties. In a deep analysis of Rhys's
texts one may even find a modicum of sympathy for the male material-
ists from Stephan in *Quartet* to Edward in *Wide Sargasso Sea*.

If women act out weakness and childishness to please men whom
they really have little or no regard for, then men are also manipulated
and exploited. Rhys fairly implies that the injustices in economic opportunities and obligations disable men *and* women and distort their relationships. Men may seem free to wander the world, while women are
confined to rooms, but in truth male freedom is only an illusion as long
as economic ties exist between genders and must be negotiated overtly
or subtly before new relationships may be begun. If women must
remain nominally faithful to their possessors, then the possessors,
though they may philander, are economically tied to the possessed as
long as they are allowed to be, or wish to remain, possessors.

Rhys's "manual" for female survival is not compatible with contemporary feminism and is not truly workable: make full use of the weapons
of "femininity" the patriarchal system has allowed or inadvertently created. That guerrilla war has not won many victories. Paradoxically,
Rhys's novels argue by implication and event against the strategy she
invokes. Her heroines never win (Le Gallez, 6).

West Indian Writer

Before writing *Wide Sargasso Sea* Rhys was aware that her West Indian
background meant little to Europeans and North Americans. But that
background provided a coded entrance for the writer into her primary
characterizations, particularly her heroines, that made it easier for her to
realize them. When Rhys wrote *Wide Sargasso Sea* she "came out of the

Caribbean closet" and displayed all her island background, knowledge, experience, and values. Consciously or subconsciously Rhys associated the fate of women in the twentieth century with that of colonials resisting control by a dominant, imperial culture.

As a colonial or ex-colonial, Rhys always considered herself an outsider in Europe. Even when she lived peripherally in Paris among the British and American expatriates who were themselves outsiders there and to their home cultures, she was an outsider. The islands were the Eden from which she had been banished for life. Dominica was the mother in whose womb she wished to, but could not hide. The Jamaican novelist John Hearne opines that in writing *Wide Sargasso Sea* Rhys had the opportunity to let her psyche run free and thus produced "a superb and audacious metaphor of so much of West Indian life."[7] It should also be noted that Rhys's upbringing in Roseau society providentially gave her skills that served her well as a beginning writer in the Paris of the 1920s. The culture of Roseau society was partly English and partly French (O'Connor, 17). Rhys learned at an early age to move between two complementary cultures with two languages. The artistic community in *arte moderne* Paris macrocosmically replicated her girlhood experience.

With *Wide Sargasso Sea* it became clear that Rhys was a multicultural writer who understood the tensions of gender conflict because she understood the tensions between colonial resistance and imperial power as well as the tension, hostility, and aggression emanating from racial, gender, and class differences.

Rhys clearly understood and brilliantly portrayed the female consciousness in the twentieth century. She left behind a motto from herself and from the Black women of the Caribbean to all women of our difficult times and the age to come: "Woman must have spunks to live in this wicked world" (*WSS*, 101).

Notes and References

Chapter One

    1. Carole Angier, *Jean Rhys: Life and Work* (Boston: Little, Brown and Co., 1990), 8–9; hereafter cited in text.
    2. Coral Ann Howells, *Jean Rhys* (New York: St. Martin's Press, 1991), 15; hereafter cited in text.
    3. Teresa F. O'Connor, *Jean Rhys: The West Indian Novels* (New York: New York University Press, 1986), 7; hereafter cited in text.
    4. David Plante, *Difficult Women: A Memoir of Three* (New York: Atheneum, 1983), 24.
    5. *The Left Bank and Other Stories* (New York: Harper and Brothers, 1927), 24; hereafter cited in text as *LB*.
    6. Arthur Mizener, *The Saddest Story: A Biography of Ford Madox Ford* (New York: World Publishing Company, 1971), 347.
    7. Diana Athill, "Jean Rhys and Her Autobiography," foreword to *Smile Please: An Unfinished Autobiography* (Berkeley: Donald S. Ellis/Creative Arts, 1982), 3; hereafter cited in the text as *Smile*.

Chapter Two

    1. Thomas F. Staley, *Jean Rhys: A Critical Study* (Austin: University of Texas Press, 1979), 21; hereafter cited in the text.
    2. Helen Tiffin, "Post-Colonial Literatures and Counter-Discourse," *Kunapipi* 9, no. 3 (1987): 19; hereafter cited in the text.
    3. Arnold E. Davidson, *Jean Rhys* (New York: Frederick Unger Publishing Company, 1985), 120; hereafter cited in the text.

Chapter Three

    1. *Quartet* (New York: Harper & Row, 1971), 13; hereafter cited in the text as *Q*.
    2. Mary Lou Emery, *Jean Rhys at "World's End": Novels of Colonial and Sexual Exile* (Austin: University of Texas Press, 1990), 112; hereafter cited in the text.
    3. Nancy R. Harrison, *Jean Rhys and the Novel as Women's Text* (Chapel Hill: University of North Carolina Press, 1988), 63; hereafter cited in the text.
    4. Helen Nebeker, *Jean Rhys: Woman in Passage: A Critical Study of the Novels of Jean Rhys* (Montreal: Eden Press, 1981), 8; hereafter cited in the text.

5. Mikhail Bakhtin, *Rabalais and His World,* trans. Hélène Iswolsky (Bloomington: Indiana University Press, 1984), 39–40.

6. Paula Le Gallez, *The Rhys Woman* (New York: St. Martin's Press, 1990), 34.

7. Thomas F. Staley, "The Emergence of a Form: Style and Consciousness in Jean Rhys's *Quartet,*" *Critical Perspectives on Jean Rhys,* ed. Pierrette M. Frickey (Washington, D.C.: Three Continents Press, 1990), 146.

8. Alicia Borinsky, "Jean Rhys: Poses of a Woman as Guest," in *The Female Body in Western Culture,* ed. Susan Rubin Suleiman (Cambridge: Harvard University Press, 1986), 301; hereafter cited in the text.

Chapter Four

1. *After Leaving Mr. Mackenzie* (New York: Harper & Row, 1931), 111; hereafter cited in the text as *ALMM.*

2. Deborah Kelly Kloepfer, *The Unspeakable Mother: Forbidden Discourse in Jean Rhys and H. D.* (Ithaca: Cornell University Press, 1989), 146; hereafter cited in the text.

Chapter Five

1. Elgin W. Mellown, *Jean Rhys: A Descriptive and Annotated Bibliography of Works and Criticism* (New York: Garland Publishing, 1984), xi; hereafter cited in the text.

2. *Voyage in the Dark* (London: André Deutsch, 1967), 164; hereafter cited in the text as *V.*

3. Louis James, "Sun Fire—Painted Fire: Jean Rhys as a Caribbean Novelist," *Critical Perspectives on Jean Rhys,* edited by Pierrette M. Frickey (Washington, D.C.: Three Continents Press, 1990), 121–22.

4. Pearl Hochstadt, "From Vulnerability to Selfhood: The Pain-Filled Affirmations of Jean Rhys," *The Jean Rhys Review* 2, no. 1 (1987): 3.

5. Elizabeth Abel, "Women and Schizophrenia: The Fiction of Jean Rhys," *Contemporary Literature* 20, no. 2 (1979): 155–58.

6. Mary Lou Emery, "The Politics of Form: Jean Rhys's Social Vision in *Voyage in the Dark* and *Wide Sargasso Sea,*" *Twentieth Century Literature* 28, no. 4 (1982P): 419; hereafter cited in the text as Emery, "Politics."

7. Jan Curtis, "Jean Rhys's *Voyage in the Dark:* A Reassessment," *Journal of Commonwealth Literature* 22, no. 1 (1987): 144; hereafter cited in the text.

8. Elaine Showalter, *A Literature of Their Own: British Women Novelists from Brontë to Lessing* (Princeton: Princeton University Press, 1977), 258.

Chapter Six

1. Arnold E. Davidson, "The Dark Is Light Enough: Affirmation from Despair in Jean Rhys's *Good Morning, Midnight,*" *Contemporary Literature* 24, no. 3 (1983): 352.

2. *Good Morning, Midnight* (London: André Deutsch, 1967), 27; hereafter cited in the text as *GMM*.

3. Marsha Z. Cummins, "Point of View in the Novels of Jean Rhys: The Effect of a Double Focus," *World Literature Written in English* 24, no. 2 (1984): 367.

Chapter Seven

1. See Sandra Gilbert and Susan Gubar, *The Madwoman in the Attic* (New Haven: Yale University Press, 1979), 360, for a discussion of Bertha as Jane Eyre's alter ego and "truest and darkest double."

2. See Jane Neide Ashcom, "Two Modernisms: The Novels of Jean Rhys," *The Jean Rhys Review* 2, no. 2 (1988): 17–27; hereafter cited in the text.

3. *Wide Sargasso Sea* (New York: W. W. Norton & Co., 1967), 28–29; hereafter cited in the text as *WSS*.

4. Thomas Loe, "Patterns of the Zombie in Jean Rhys's *Wide Sargasso Sea,*" *World Literature Written in English* 31, no. 1 (1991): 40.

5. Thorunn Lonsdale, "The Female Child in the Fiction of Jean Rhys," *Commonwealth Essays and Studies* 15, no. 1 (1992): 62; hereafter cited in the text.

6. Lucy Wilson, " 'Women [sic] Must Have Spunks': Jean Rhys's West Indian Outcasts," *Critical Perspectives on Jean Rhys*, ed. Pierrette M. Frickey (Washington, D.C.: Three Continents Press, 1990), 72.

7. Nancy J. Leigh, "Mirror, Mirror: The Development of Female Identity in Jean Rhys's Fiction," *World Literature Written in English* 25, no. 2 (1985): 273–77; hereafter cited in the text. See also Lori Lawson, "Mirror and Madness: A Lacanian Analysis of the Feminine Subject in *Wide Sargasso Sea*," *Jean Rhys Review* 4, no. 2 (1991): 19–27, for a Lacanian reading of the mirror image as identification and objectifying artifact in *Wide Sargasso Sea*, and Freya Johnson, "The Male Gaze and the Struggle against Patriarchy in *Jane Eyre* and *Wide Sargasso Sea*," *Jean Rhys Review* 5, no. 1–2 (1992): 22–30, for the mirror as a site of struggle against patriarchy in both novels.

Chapter Eight

1. A. C. Morrell, "The World of Jean Rhys's Short Stories," *Critical Perspectives on Jean Rhys*, ed. Pierrette M. Frickey (Washington, D.C.: Three Continents Press, 1990), 102.

2. *Tigers Are Better-Looking* (London: André Deutsch, 1968), 32; hereafter cited in the text as *Tigers*.

3. *Sleep It Off, Lady* (New York: Harper & Row, 1976), 22; hereafter cited in the text as *Sleep*.

Chapter Nine

1. Carol R. Hagley, "Aging in the Fiction of Jean Rhys," *World Literature Written in English* 28, no. 1 (1988): 124.

2. *My Day* (New York: Frank Hallman, 1975), 8; hereafter cited in the text as *MD*.

3. John Updike, "Dark Smile, Devilish Saints," *The New Yorker* 56, no. 82 (11 August 1980) as cited in *Critical Perspectives on Jean Rhys,* ed. Pierrette M. Frickey (Washington, D.C.: Three Continents Press, 1990), 207.

4. Adrienne Rich, *Of Women Born: Motherhood as Experience and Institution* (New York: W. W. Norton & Co., 1976), 226.

Chapter Ten

1. A. Alvarez, "The Best Living English Novelist," *New York Times Book Review,* 17 March 1974.

2. Noel Annan, *Our Age: English Intellectuals Between the World Wars—A Group Portrait* (New York: Random House, 1990), 290.

3. For a related discussion of the contemporary theorist Julia Kristeva's argument that the liberation of women from their marginal position in society will only be accomplished by the production of alternative nonhierarchical discourses in language, semiotics, psychology, psychoanalysis, and sociology, see Ann Rosalind Jones, "Writing the Body: Toward an Understanding of *l'écriture féminine,*" in *Feminist Criticism and Social Change: Sex, Class, and Race in Literature and Culture,* ed. Judith Newton and Deborah Rosenfelt (New York: Methuen, 1985), 87–88.

4. V. S. Naipaul, "Without a Dog's Chance: *After Leaving Mr. Mackenzie,*" *Critical Perspectives on Jean Rhys,* ed. Pierrette M. Frickey (Washington, D.C.: Three Continents Press, 1990), 58.

5. Pearl Hochstadt, "From Vulnerability to Selfhood: The Pain-Filled Affirmations of Jean Rhys," *Jean Rhys Review* 2, no. 1 (1987): 3.

6. Veronica Marie Gregg, "Jean Rhys and Modernism: A Different Voice," *The Jean Rhys Review* 1, no. 2 (1987): 33.

7. John Hearne, "*The Wide Sargasso Sea:* A West Indian Reflection," *Cornhill* Magazine (Summer, 1974): 325.

Selected Bibliography

PRIMARY SOURCES

Novels

After Leaving Mr. Mackenzie. London: Cape, 1931; New York: Knopf, 1931; London: André Deutsch, 1969; Hammondsworth, Middlesex: Penguin 1971; New York: Harper & Row, 1982.

The Complete Novels of Jean Rhys. New York: W. W. Norton & Co., 1985.

The Early Novels of Jean Rhys. London: André Deutsch, 1984.

Good Morning, Midnight. London: Constable, 1939; London: André Deutsch, 1967; Hammondsworth, Middlesex: Penguin, 1969; New York: Harper & Row, 1970.

Postures. London: Chatto & Windus, 1928. Reprinted as *Quartet.* New York: Simon & Schuster, 1929; London: André Deutsch, 1969; New York: Harper & Row, 1971.

Voyage in the Dark. London: Constable, 1934; New York: Morrow, 1935; London: André Deutsch, 1967; Hammondsworth, Middlesex: Penguin, 1969; New York: W. W. Norton & Co., 1982.

Wide Sargasso Sea. London: André Deutsch, 1966; New York: W. W. Norton & Co., 1967.

Short Stories

The Collected Short Stories. New York: W. W. Norton & Co., 1987.

The Left Bank and Other Stories. London: Cape, 1927; New York: Harper and Brothers, 1927; New York: Books for Libraries Press, 1970.

Sleep It Off, Lady. London: André Deutsch, 1976; New York: Harper & Row, 1976; Hammondsworth, Middlesex: Penguin, 1981.

Tigers Are Better-Looking. London: André Deutsch, 1968; New York: Harper & Row, 1974.

Autobiographical Writing

My Day. New York: Frank Hallman, 1975.

Smile Please: An Unfinished Autobiography. London: André Deutsch, 1979; New York: Harper & Row, 1980; Hammondsworth, Middlesex: Penguin, 1981.

Letters

Jean Rhys's Letters 1931–1966. Edited by Francis Wyndham and Diana Melly. London: André Deutsch, 1984; Hammondsworth, Middlesex: Penguin, 1985; reprinted as *The Letters of Jean Rhys*, New York: Viking, 1984.

SECONDARY SOURCES

Bibliography

Mellown, Elgin W. *Jean Rhys: A Descriptive and Annotated Bibliography of Works and Criticism.* New York: Garland Publishing, 1984. Invaluable research tool up to 1984. Contains an excellent brief introduction to Rhys's life and work.

Books and Parts of Books

Angier, Carole. *Jean Rhys: Life and Work.* London: André Deutsch, 1990; Boston: Little, Brown and Co., 1990. Exemplary literary biography and critical introduction to Rhys. Corrects much misinformation about Rhys's life.

Benstock, Shari. *Women of the Left Bank: Paris 1900–1940.* Austin: University of Texas Press, 1987. Presents Rhys as one of 22 women writers who created the Left Bank's feminine identity. Fine background study for Rhys's early work.

Borinsky, Alicia. "Jean Rhys: Poses of a Woman as Guest." In *The Female Body in Western Culture,* edited by Susan Suleiman, 288–302. Cambridge: Harvard University Press, 1986.

Davidson, Arnold E. *Jean Rhys.* New York: Unger, 1985. Useful and insightful short introduction to Rhys's work.

Emery, Mary Lou. *Jean Rhys at "World's End": Novels of Colonial and Sexual Exile.* Austin: University of Texas Press, 1990. Powerful study depicting Rhys's heroines as occupiers of marginal spaces.

Gregg, Veronica Marie. *Jean Rhys's Historical Imagination: Reading and Writing the Creole.* Chapel Hill: University of North Carolina Press, 1995. Reads Rhys as a West Indian Creole seeking a place and an identity in a rejecting society.

Harrison, Nancy Rebecca. *Jean Rhys and the Novel as Women's Text.* Chapel Hill: University of North Carolina Press, 1988. Emphasizes the subtextuality and the world of women's speech in Rhys's writing.

Howells, Coral Ann. *Jean Rhys.* New York: St. Martin's Press, 1991. Locates Rhys's contribution to the poetics of female space within the canon of high modernism.

James, Louis. *Jean Rhys*. London: Longman, 1978. Early study of Rhys as a
colonial exile writing within a developing tradition of post-colonial
Caribbean discourse.
————. "Sun Fire—Painted Fire: Jean Rhys as a Caribbean Novelist." In *Critical Perspectives on Jean Rhys,* edited by Pierrette M. Frickey, 118–28.
Washington, D.C.: Three Continents Press, 1990. Compares and contrasts "Anna Morgan's" and Jean Rhys's Dominica and England. Points
out the interrelatedness of *Voyage in the Dark* and *Wide Sargasso Sea.*
Kloepfer, Deborah Kelly. *The Unspeakable Mother: Forbidden Discourse in Jean
Rhys and H.D.* Ithaca: Cornell University Press, 1989. Depicts the Rhys
canon as a daughter's speaking out the pain from the loss of the absent
mother figure. Foregrounds mother/daughter relationship and discourse.
Le Gallez, Paula. *The Rhys Woman.* New York: St. Martin's Press, 1990. A
reader-response interpretation of the iterative heroine in Rhys's work.
Separates autobiography from style.
Morrell, A. C. "The World of Jean Rhys's Short Stories." In *Critical Perspectives
on Jean Rhys,* edited by Pierrette M. Frickey, 95–102. Washington, D.C.:
Three Continents Press, 1990. Excellent brief overview of Rhys's achievement as a short story writer.
Nebeker, Helen. *Jean Rhys, Woman in Passage: A Critical Study of the novels of Jean
Rhys.* Montreal: Eden Press, 1981. Feminist, archetype-exploring reading
of the Rhys canon, disconnecting it from the autobiographical sources
and focusing on psychological models.
O'Connor, Teresa F. *Jean Rhys: The West Indian Novels.* New York: New York
University Press, 1986. Folds Rhys's Dominican experience into *Voyage
in the Dark* and *Wide Sargasso Sea.*
Plante, David. *Difficult Women: A Memoir of Three.* New York: Atheneum,
1983. Portrays Rhys in extreme old age trying to cope with fame, illness,
a continuing desire to write, and fear of death.
Staley, Thomas F. *Jean Rhys: A Critical Study.* Austin: University of Texas Press,
1979. Ground-breaking critical work. Situates Rhys as an original and
distinctive voice in the modernist tradition.
————. "The Emergence of a Form: Style and Consciousness in Jean Rhys's
Quartet." In *Critical Perspectives on Jean Rhys,* edited by Pierrette M.
Frickey, 129–47. Washington, D.C.: Three Continents Press, 1990.
Detailed examination of Rhys's stylistic accomplishment in *Quartet.*

Articles

Abel, Elizabeth. "Women and Schizophrenia: The Fiction of Jean Rhys." *Contemporary Literature* 20, no. 2 (1979): 155–77. Adapts R. D. Laing's theories of ontological security and schizophrenia to account for the perversely self-destructive behavior of Rhys's heroines.

Ashcom, Jane Neide. "Two Modernisms: The Novels of Jean Rhys." *The Jean Rhys Review* 2, no. 2 (1988): 17–27. Demonstrates how Rhys's first four novels conform to early modernist expressionism, while *Wide Sargasso Sea* employs the mythic dimensions of later modernism.

Brandmark, Wendy. "The Power of the Victim: A Study of *Quartet, After Leaving Mr. Mackenzie,* and *Voyage in the Dark* by Jean Rhys." *Kunapipi* 8, no. 2 (1986): 21–29. Discusses the victimization of the Rhys heroine by parental figures.

Cummins, Marsha Z. "Point of View in the Novels of Jean Rhys: The Effect of a Double Focus." *World Literature Written in English* 24, no. 2 (1984): 359–73. Discusses the use of focus shifts to create emotional environments of humiliation and determinism in order to legitimize the paranoia of the Rhys heroine.

Curtis, Jan. "Jean Rhys's *Voyage in the Dark:* A Reassessment." *Journal of Commonwealth Literature* 22, no. 1 (1987): 144–58. Rejects Freudian, Jungian, Feminist theoretical views of *Voyage in the Dark* in favor of an image-based interpretation of the text for a psychological analysis of experience.

Davidson, Arnold E. "The Dark Is Light Enough: Affirmation from Despair in Jean Rhys's *Good Morning, Midnight.*" *Contemporary Literature* 24, no. 3 (1983): 349–64. Sees the controversial ending of *Good Morning, Midnight* as an ambiguous affirmation of the heroine's life and of existence itself.

Emery, Mary Lou. "The Politics of Form: Jean Rhys's Social Vision in *Voyage in the Dark* and *Wide Sargasso Sea.*" *Twentieth Century Literature* 28, no. 4 (1982): 418–30. Emphasizes the violence, sexual barter, social exclusion, psychological assault, and exile of poverty as demonstrated by Rhys through modernist techniques.

Gregg, Veronica Marie. "Jean Rhys and Modernism: A Different Voice." *The Jean Rhys Review* 1, no. 2 (1987): 30–46. Outlines Rhys's connection to modernism and her relationship to other women writers of her time. Locates Rhys in the modernist spectrum.

Hagley, Carol R. "Aging in the Fiction of Jean Rhys." *World Literature Written in English* 28, no. 1 (1988): 115–25. Sees aging as one of several ways in which Rhys depicts the alienation and exile of people from society.

Hochstadt, Pearl. "From Vulnerability to Selfhood: The Pain-Filled Affirmations of Jean Rhys." *The Jean Rhys Review* 2, no. 1 (1987): 2–6. Sees Rhys's novels as a product of an obsessive struggle to come to terms with women's alienation and vulnerability.

Johnson, Freya. "The Male Gaze and the Struggle against Patriarchy in *Jane Eyre* and *Wide Sargasso Sea.*" *The Jean Rhys Review* 5, no. 1–2 (1992): 22–30. Locates the mirror as a site of the struggle against patriarchy in both texts. Jane and Antoinette encounter controlling patriarchal values in the glass, not in a dissimilar way to their encounter with them in that other reflection, language.

Lawson, Lori. "Mirror and Madness: A Lacanian Analysis of the Feminine Subject in *Wide Sargasso Sea.*" *The Jean Rhys Review* 4, no. 2 (1991): 19–27. Examines the "mirror stage" in Antoinette's psychological development, from narcissism to objectification.

Leigh, Nancy J. "Mirror, Mirror: The Development of Female Identity in Jean Rhys's Fiction." *World Literature Written in English* 25, no. 2 (1985): 273–77. Depicts Rhys's women as victims, economically insecure, powerless, and turned into sexual objects to pleasure men, while mirrors reflect their disassociation and instability.

Loe, Thomas. "Patterns of the Zombie in Jean Rhys's *Wide Sargasso Sea.*" *World Literature Written in English* 31, no. 1 (1991): 34–42. Establishes the zombie as a powerful West Indian metaphor for the powerlessness and displacement of women in transit from one culture to another.

Lonsdale, Thorunn. "The Female Child in the Fiction of Jean Rhys." *Commonwealth Essays and Studies* 15, no. 1 (1992): 61- 68. Concise essay isolating the significance of the Caribbean background of the Rhys female child in *Wide Sargasso Sea* and the short stories.

Morris, Merwin. "Oh, Give the Girl a Chance: Jean Rhys and *Voyage in the Dark.*" *Journal of West Indian Literature* 3, no. 2 (1989): 1–8. Discusses the original drafts, various rewrites, and the creative process in the production of *Voyage in the Dark*.

Tiffin, Helen. "Post-Colonial Literatures and Counter-Discourse." *Kunapipi* 9, no. 3 (1987): 17–34. Discusses post-colonial literature as a cross-cultural product. Sees Rhys in confrontation with what is British.

Index

153

The Author

Sanford Sternlicht, professor emeritus of theater and English at the State University of New York at Oswego, is currently part-time professor of English at Syracuse University. He is the author the following books: *Gull's Way* (1961), poetry; *Love in Pompeii* (1967), poetry; *The Black Devil of the Bayous* (1970), history (with E. M. Jameson); *John Webster's Imagery and the Webster Canon* (1972); *McKinley's Bulldog: The Battleship Oregon* (1977), history; *John Masefield* (1977); *C. S. Forester* (1981); *USF Constellation: Yankee Racehorse* (1981), history (with E. M. Jameson); *Padraic Colum* (1985); *John Galsworthy* (1987); *R. F. Delderfield* (1988); *Stevie Smith* (1990); *Stephen Spender* (1992); *Siegfried Sassoon* (1993); *All Things Herriot: James Herriot and His Peaceable Kingdom* (1995).

Sternlicht has edited *Selected Short Stories of Padraic Colum* (1985), *Selected Plays of Padraic Colum* (1986), *Selected Poems of Padraic Colum* (1989), and *In Search of Stevie Smith* (1991). His articles on subjects from Shakespeare to Graham Greene have appeared in numerous journals, and his poetry can be found in more than three hundred publications. He received the *Writer Magazine* New Poets Award in 1960, a poetry fellowship from the Poetry Society of America, and several State University of New York Research Foundation fellowships and grants. In the 1960s Sternlicht was Leverhulme Visiting Fellow at the University of York, England.

The Editor

Kinley E. Roby is professor of English at Northeastern University. He is the Twentieth-Century Field Editor of the Twayne English Authors Series, Series Editor of Twayne's Critical History of British Dramas, and General Editor of Twayne's Women and Literature Series. He has written books on Arnold Bennett, Edward VII, and Joyce Cary and edited a collection of essays on T. S. Eliot. He makes his home in Sudbury, Massachusetts.